MIND THE BRAND GAP

A study of
Competing Brand Identities,
Human Biases
and Why You MUST FIRE
your HR team

Printed in the United Kingdom

ISBN : 978-1-9996225-4-1
eISBN: 978-1-9996225-5-8

CONTENTS

To my wife Diana and my daughter Beatrice, with love

FOREWORD

I have started to write this book with the goal of helping brands and organizations to debunk the myths on corporate identity that are so alive in many of today's business models. Now, more than ever it is time for both brands and organizations i.e. franchising agreements to acknowledge the futility of developing and promoting brand identities that are most often not reflective of the reality and perceptions on the ground. Wasted money, employee turnover, customer defection. These are only few of the many effects, and resources wasted by inefficient brand "architects" and managers or leaders on researching the "brand values", printing nice corporate posters and collateral materials, delivering employee brand ambassadors programs, motivational speeches or expensive re-branding campaigns. Indeed, brands go to extreme lengths to promote the idea that employees and customers should excitedly embrace its ideal images, live by or promote its values almost religiously. The problem is that these brand identity programs simply aren't working. Brands operate under the assumption that employees are some sort of a "blank slate" which can be written and overwritten on over and over again with new values and brand behaviors. Moreover, brands seem to believe that all they need doing is take some brand values as ingredients, drop it in a highly complex system, mix it continually and get a aesthetically pleasing, consistent brand identity that employees, customers and other stakeholders will rally to excitedly live, breathe and adhere to.

And yet, employees, customers and other stakeholders are anything but empty recipients and they have their own values, perceptions, characteristics and goals. They can certainly see beyond the fog of corporate messages, and feel the reality on the ground. And, large gaps between communicated and experienced brand identity lead employees to the predictable outcome of rejecting brand messages. In fact, the higher the gap, the more stubbornly employees reject the corporate message. And the more the brand pushes, the more employees resist and give way to a cascade of secondary effects: customers experience the gaps, form an image based on their experience of the brand, which in time impacts brand reputation, and ultimately depletes revenues and profits. This is turn leads to pressures on protecting profits, further affecting employee perceptions, and the process starts all over again in a cycle that further increases identity gaps.

I personally experienced some of these issues around brand identity and the various factors impacting its success during the well publicized re-branding exercise of a major hotel brand I was working for at the time. In the past, that particular brand owned most of its hotel properties, which allowed it to hold a very tight grip on the process of delivering the brand identity, and how it was promoted and implemented within the business. In a nutshell, the brand controlled the message and the implementation, which enhanced the consistency and coherence of its overall image. However, like most industries after the credit crunch, hospitality has faithfully followed the trend of increased efficiency at the expense of employee motivation and quality of service. Given the need of increased efficiency this well known brand accelerated the process of offloading fixed costs, in this case hotels, in a strategy which shifted its direction from owning the properties to focusing on their core capability, which was building and developing brands. The answer to this shift was a franchising strategy, a strategy adopted since then by most major hotel brands. So, on one side we have a brand focusing on writing nice statements, printing posters, promoting ideal values, advocating employee commitment and motivation, investment in staff, and great customer satisfaction. On the other side, we have hotel owners whose primary goal was making money, improving revenues and reducing costs. In brief, the brand is focused on delivering an ideal image while hotel owners have their own goals, styles of managing the business, and own company cultures. The fact of the matter is that the brand had already lost control, and this was never going to work. For example, after economic meltdown in 2007, hotel owners came to the belief that their commitment to brand identity was being overshadowed by the price sensitivity of customers. Understandably, then they focused on reducing the wage bill and investment in hotels as a priority in increasing efficiency, acknowledging that, given the precarious state of the economy, customers would trade service quality for price savings. Organizations restructured themselves, flattened their reporting structures, and in many cases centralized their operations. Jobs were lost; roles were combined or eliminated altogether. There was still the problem of reducing salaries and wages though, and owners achieved this goal by systematically deskilling their workforce and shifting the bargaining power from the professional hotelier to the hotel owner. This outcome was achieved through leveraging two particular trends: outsourcing and automation. One example that underlines the impact of outsourcing in hotels concerns the housekeeping teams of many branded hotels. Previously, the typical hotel had employed housekeeping team members directly. However, the need for increased efficiency meant that that system gave way to a new business model; third party companies were formed with the objective of convincing hotels that it was cheaper to outsource than to manage the housekeeping function in-house. How was better efficiency achieved? The catch is that most often the very same housekeeping team members that were employed by the hotel directly were now being forced to choose between losing their income through being made redundant by the hotel or working for the agency. We now have the same team, in the same hotel, working for lower wages and under increased strain to increase productivity. To sum up, hotel owners had to either continue their commitment to employee and customer satisfaction in line with the brand identity, or make employees redundant, enjoy services of similar quality from an agency that re-employed their former employees, and save both on wages and on the financial responsibilities associated with employing housekeepers directly. Of course, the only person disadvantaged was the housekeeper, who now experienced increased workload and lower wages. Such examples can be easily identified in literally every industry you can think of. Take the translation and interpreting field as another example. Previously, experienced linguists worked directly for the Ministry of Justice and the Police. In a drastic attempt to reduce costs, consequently at the expense of quality, the government organized a bidding process and granted contracts for these services to the third party companies that promised the highest savings, with no consideration of how the savings were to be achieved. How did these companies achieve the savings? By forcing professional translators and interpreters to make a choice: work for them at dramatically reduced rates and disadvantageous conditions, or be replaced by lower skilled, inexperienced people who often had no prior knowledge or understanding of the field, let alone the legal implications and obligations involved. Many experienced linguists resisted, and many gave in. Regardless of their choice, the results were mainly felt by the experienced linguists, who saw their income drastically reduced, and by defendants, who experienced failures in the provision of accurate and professional language services.

Another trend I introduced earlier is automation, one example that comes to mind in hospitality is the testing and adoption of self-check-in/check-out stations in many branded hotels. Now, the witty, smart and educated front desk receptionist was being replaced with lower-skilled hostesses, who attended to multiple check-in/check-out machines simultaneously. This certainly achieved the goal of reducing both staffing levels and wages at the same time. The situation is symptomatic of most industries. Only last week I entered my local Morrisons store to find that one more human-manned check-out stations had been removed, bringing the number of self-check-out points to 10, against eight human-manned check-outs. Of course, one visibly worn down member of staff was managing the whole 10 self-check-out machines. And looking at the manned checkout stations, employees look anything but happy to be there. Similarly, my local Tesco Express boasts two human-manned check-out points vs. three self-check-outs, and my local Sainsbury's has two human-manned check-outs vs. four self-check-outs. Perhaps Uber, a company that succeeded in leveraging technology to make the expensive taxi trip in London more affordable, provides the best example of how the outsourcing–automation trend unfolds. You can easily argue that Uber successfully reduced trip fares by outsourcing their services to taxi drivers who owned their own car; in fact, to the best of my knowledge, Uber owns no cabs at all. Various scandals over the years have pointed to the fact that savings in fares come at the expense of lower incomes for drivers, who seem to have resigned themselves to earning less than in their pre-Uber life. Overall, I cannot imagine these employees thinking very excitedly about the values of the brand and its identity.

Going back to hospitality, I decided to carry out a case study for several reasons. Firstly, I had direct access to the brand. Secondly, the brand was going through a major re-branding with a significant budget, which should have guaranteed its success and the implications were considerable both for customers and employees. Thirdly, throughout my career I was fortunate to work for and conduct research within a variety of hotels within the brand, which ensured that I could probe my findings first hand. Fourthly, I was puzzled by the visible inconsistencies between the brand identity and its actual manifestation in real life. The most obvious example being the wide range of results achieved by branded hotels in areas like employee surveys or guest satisfaction surveys. Specifically, if the brand identity was unitary then these results should have been relatively similar as well. However this is never the case. Wide gaps of corporate identity perceptions between the various hotel properties are found on a regular basis. Most importantly, the gaps seem to fluctuate depending on the owners of the hotels: some franchisees excelled at employee engagement and guest satisfaction, and other failed miserably.

Finally, I believe that hospitality is representative of other current industries in terms of variety of goals i.e. revenue, profit, market share, employee surveys, customers satisfaction surveys, H&S etc. Indeed organizations in most industries aim in some way or another to achieve one or more of these KPIs. It is therefore important to point out that while hospitality industry represented the case study of this book, the examples above confirm that this trend is pertinent to most industries nowadays. Indeed, we could have just as well have chosen a company operating in retail, digital marketing, translation and interpreting and so forth.

Going back to the brand that formed the object of this study, the re-branding exercise did very little to changing the wide range of perceptions of the brand by both employees and customers. Indeed, there were, and still are large gaps in terms of employee survey results throughout the brand, and the same goes for customer satisfaction survey as well. The friction between the brand and the hotel owner is still there and growing. For example, if you attended a General Managers meeting of many franchising companies it would not be uncommon to hear the CEO or Owner being proud of "pushing back" the brand on its requirements for investment, by leveraging the portfolio of hotels owned by these franchisees. As you have probably guessed, these companies are well underperforming against the brand key performance indicators, and are generally widely acknowledged for strategies of cutting corners in everything they do. By contrast, while taking one of the many mandatory training sessions ran by the brand, you will often hear trainers claiming victory over hotel owners and you guessed it..."pushing back" on them. And in the middle, employees must live by and passionately embrace brand values, and do so with significantly less resources, less support or a lack of genuine concern for their development and motivation.

My hope is that this book will provide many of these companies, brands, leaders and managers with an opportunity to reflect over the damaging impact of these inconsistencies on building strong brand identities. You will also be introduced to the different and competing facets of the brand identity, and the relationships between them. The terms brand identity and corporate identity are interchangeable; for the remaining part of the book I will be referring to brand identity as corporate identity. You will also learn about some unexpected factors impacting corporate identity, recruitment practices in particular is one factor that many consider more of a management rather than a marketing practice. As I will argue though, this is a gross misunderstanding and one primary cause of so many failed corporate identity programs. Finally, we will discuss the technological trends and solutions to the problem represented by recruitment. Trends including Artificial Intelligence, Machine Learning, Big Data or VR will be introduced into the mix to argue the case for removing decision from the highly inefficient, biased and overconfident HR professional, manager or leader.

If you have been reading my previous books you would have got accustomed with my plain, straightforward language. On this occasion I am sorry to disappoint, you will find this book a bit different. The book is based on two studies I have carried out while studying for my MBA and MA in Marketing & Innovation. As such, the book is meant to be slightly more academic both in terms of language and its structure. With this in mind, I am very confident that if you read it through you will thoroughly enjoy the conversation, and gain some very surprising insights as a leader or manager.

The book is structured in four parts:

Part 1 – A study on competing identities within brands and organizations, and primary factors that affect it: corporate identity, organizational identity, corporate image, organizational image, corporate reputation, bi-polar identities, sub-cultures, corporate structure, corporate strategy, leadership and recruitment practices.

Part 2 – A study on the efficiency of brands in recruiting the right "brand people". Various human biases affecting recruitment decisions will be discussed to support the idea that recruitment is a primary cause of corporate identity misalignment. You will be introduced to biases such as first impressions, overconfidence, halo effects, gender of the recruiter, stereotypes, mood of recruiters, willpower, priming, attractiveness of candidates to name just a few. However, this is not a book about recruitment per se, and as such previous studies on human biases are briefly introduced and discussed in relation to findings of the study on a sample of 11 managers, as opposed to discussing each bias in detail.

Part 3 – A discussion on why organizations are better off removing decisions on recruitment from the hands of managers and HR professionals. We will discuss technological forces impacting the field of Search Engine Optimization to argue that Artificial Intelligence/Machine Learning algorithms will do a far better job than humans at recruiting the right people for the brand. Some areas we will look at include AI, Machine Learning, Virtual Reality, Augmented Reality to name just a few. Several case studies will be introduced underlining how companies already make use of these technologies to improve their recruitment process.

Part 4 – Recommendations for further research

Finally, a small piece of advice to the impatient reader: if you are not particularly keen on reading about the methodology of the studies introduced in Part 1 and Part 2 of the book, you can easily jump back and forward between the chapters that are discussing the concepts, findings and conclusions of the studies.

I hope you will enjoy the ride...let's get started!

PART 1.
THE MANY FACETS OF BRAND IDENTITY

CHAPTER 1.
SUMMARY

This study investigated the factors influencing corporate identity perceptions by employees, and their commitment to brands. The results are based on a case study of a well-known international hotel brand that completed its re-branding process. The study focused on analyzing the information communicated through the company intranet and websites, an existing employee survey and eighteen in-depth interviews with employees at two hotels of the brand, managed by the same company. The two hotels are of different size, in different locations and have different operational challenges and structure. The hotel in London is the largest hotel of the brand within the UK and a flagship for the company. The second hotel is smaller and in a location outside London.

The study confirmed several findings by previous writers. First, a large corporate-organizational gap was found within the brand. Then, the study revealed multiple identities and sub-cultures within the brand at national, divisional, unit, departmental, sub-departmental, and sub-cultures within sub-cultures, which supports the idea that achieving a unitary corporate identity is virtually impossible. The study also found that strategy, corporate structure, leadership and shared values of employees/brand/hotel owners affected employee perceptions and commitment to the brand. Bi-polar identities were found to have little impact on influencing employee perceptions, while corporate image, organizational image, and corporate reputation were most likely to influence employee perceptions of the brand only when considered in conjunction with employee perceptions of the organizational identity. Overall, organizational identity was found to have the highest influence on corporate identity both directly and indirectly, as indicated above. In order to ensure the success of corporate identity programs, brands must pay increased attention to understanding and aligning corporate and organizational identities.

CHAPTER 2.
INTRODUCTION

2.1 Why This Research?

Eales, quoted by Melewar and Saunders (1998), predicted in early 1990 that "a multinational company's personality and identity will become the biggest factor in consumer choice between its products and those of another". Nowadays, most writers (Balmer and Gray, 2000; Kiriakidou and Millward, 2000; Hatch and Shultz, 1997, etc.) would agree that in today's business environment with fast technological advancement, deregulation, globalization, increased competition and public expectations for corporate social responsiveness (Balmer and Gray, 2000), the predictions by Eales came true. Corporate identity has become an essential strategic tool, "many organizations striving to develop a distinct and recognizable identity," (Melewar and Karaosmanoglu, 2006).

Yet, before "selling" corporate identity to an external audience, organizations generally acknowledge that they must sell it to their own employees, whose role in "living the brand" is crucial (Kiriakidou and Millward, 2000; Hatch and Shultz, 1997; Gotsi and Adriopoulous, 2007; Gotsi and Adriopoulous, 2008; de Chernatony and Cottam, 2008, etc.). This is why most organizations use internal marketing activities to gain employee commitment to corporate identity, in the hope that employees will mirror this identity to external stakeholders. However, despite significant investment, and internal marketing activities, most studies (Kiriakidou and Millward, 2000; Gotsi and Adriopoulous, 2007; Gotsi and Adriopoulous, 2008, etc.) found large gaps between how the organization presented itself and its perceptions by employees. These findings raise concerns regarding the efficacy of corporate identity programs. Despite the efforts of organizations, employees generally perceive organizations differently than wanted. External stakeholders receive their perceptions of the company in their day-to-day experiences with employees, thus it is crucial that employees adopted the correct corporate identity.

It is important to understand what are the factors affecting employees' perceptions of corporate identity. Understanding these factors will help organizations to improve the efficacy of corporate identity programs, manage and improve their "ability to create and sustain employee behaviors that allow organizations to perform differently from their rivals," (de Chernatony and Cottam, 2008).

This study is focused on a well-known international hotel brand that completed a major re-branding. The research investigated if employees bought into the new corporate identity and brand values, and what the factors influencing their perceptions of the brand identity were. While reviewing previous research, a large number of studies on corporate identity was found. A theoretical study by Harris and de Chernatony (2001) proposed a series of factors affecting corporate identity, and Melewar and Karaosmanoglu (2006) empirically analyzed factors affecting corporate identity. However, I was not able to find a comprehensive study that analyzed the various factors thought to influence employees' perceptions of corporate identity. Some studies focused on employee and management opinions, some were focusing solely on views by management teams, while others focused on employees and used quantitative methods of research exclusively. Hence, a decision was made to employing a different approach to research: semi-structured, in-depth interviews with employees at two hotels within the same brand, managed by the same company, and yet with completely different characteristics (size, number of employees, occupancy levels, mix of customers, location, etc.). Similarly to previous studies (Kiriakidou and Millward, 2000; Gotsi and Adriopoulous, 2008) a research of corporate communications through media, websites, internet, internal marketing materials, etc., was found appropriate to surveying the corporate identity, which was then compared to secondary data from an existing employee survey. This approach revealed employees' perceptions within the brand, the level of alignment between corporate and organizational identities, and the level of commitment to the brand identity.

2.2 Aims and Objectives

Previous studies proposed various factors as influencing corporate identity programs. The overall aim of the study was to further understand the impact of those factors on employee perceptions of corporate identity, and on their commitment to live by and support corporate identity. The research focused on the investigation of the following factors:

1. Organizational identity

2. Existent sub-cultures within organizations

3. Corporate image

4. Organizational image

5. Bi-polar identities

6. Corporate reputation

7. Corporate structure

8. Corporate strategy

9. Leadership

10. Recruitment Practices

Let's get started!

2.3 Concept of Identity: Definition and Beginnings

Longman's Dictionary of Contemporary English (2003) defines identity as "to recognize something or discover exactly what it is, what its nature or origin is, etc.,.... the qualities and attitudes that a person or group of people have that make them different from other people or groups".

And, the first organized identity program was suggested by Ollins (1994) as Napoleon Bonaparte's coronation as Emperor of the French Republic in 1804. Shortly afterward, Napoleon introduced names, badges, titles representing the Empire, Almoners, Princes, High Constables, etc., uniforms, symbols, and colors while numerous painters captured Napoleon's victories and successes. All these actions successfully changed the culture of the Republic into a "hero worship" culture (Ollins, 20-21: 1994). We could call it a "re-branding" of the French state. Hence, the concepts of identity initially revolved around creating new visual clues, symbols, and communication.

2.4 From National Identity to Corporate Identity

As Ollins (23:1994) observed, modern corporations are as complex as any other nation and face similar challenges. The concept of corporate identity had initially been introduced in the 1960s, first in the US and later in the UK [Balmer and Greyser (2003) quoted by He and Balmer (2007)] with Lipincot and Marguiles (1957) being acknowledged by Cornelissen and Elving (2003) as first to attribute the name "corporate identity" to logos and symbols of organizations, as a way of "identifying the organization to third parties". Since then, corporate identity has focused on external audiences. An attempt is made by organizations to use graphic design, logos, company house style or visual identification to make these organizations more fashionable, contemporary in the marketplace and to change organizational strategy, culture and communications (Kiriakidou and Millward, 2000; van Riel and Balmer, 1997).

For example, Selame and Selame (1975) quoted by Melewar, Bassett and Simoes (2006) defined corporate identity as "...the firm's visual statement to the world of who and what the company is—of how the company views itself – and therefore has a great deal to do with how the world views the company", Marguiles (1977) quoted by Balmer (2008) defined corporate identity as "the ways a company chooses to identify itself to all its stakeholders, especially through corporate visual identity", while Carter (1982) quoted by Melewar, Bassett, and Simoes (2006) defined corporate identity as "the logo or brand image of a company and all other visual manifestations of the identity of the company". However, Millward (1995) quoted by Kiriakidou and Millward (2000) noticed that corporate identity has been long understood "merely at the artefactual level (i.e. symbols, statements of philosophy and annual reports), without consideration of the social psychological reality of the organization or its everyday modus operandi". Melewar and Karaosmanoglu (2006) quote Balmer (1995) to explain that "...everything the organization does will in some way communicate the organization's identity", an idea also sustained by Ollins (1989) quoted by van Rekom (1997) who emphasized that "everything an organization does, makes, and sells, everything it says, writes down or displays should contribute to the construction of its identity". And Kiriakidou and Millward (2000), in line with work from other academics (Hatch and Shultz, 1997; Melewar and Karaosmanoglu, 2006; Markwick and Fill, 1997; van Rekom, 1997; Olutayo and Melewar, 2007, etc.) argue that organizations represent much more than symbols or marks of recognition. More than just a visual identity, it represents the ways the organizations conduct their business, the way they think, feel, behave or interface with external stakeholders through their employees. Finally, Hatch and Shultz (1997) conclude that corporate identity is "a function of leadership", while Kiriakidou and Millward (2000) further explained that corporate identity is focused on what the organization aspires to become, based on the vision and goals of its leadership.

2.5 Corporate Identity: Does It Matter?

Reflecting on the increased number of corporate identity studies, Bernstein (2009) concludes that while historically corporate identity was rarely sold to the public, nowadays "buying the company has become a prerequisite to buying the brand". Melewar and Saunders (1998) confirmed that todays' customers "buy" the company making the product: its character, its size, its identity and the confidence it inspires. Some benefits of successfully managing the corporate identity include developing a reputation for high-quality goods/services and social/environmental responsibility, a good financial performance and attracting support from financial markets, positive working environment (Melewar and Karaosmanoglu, 2006; Melewar, Bassett and Simoes, 2006), attracting and retaining high performing employees, customers or shareholders to the company and achieving strategic alliances (Holtzhausen and Fourie, 2008; Melewar, Bassett and Simoes, 2006). Melewar and Bains (2002) emphasize that corporate identity is essential in creating a distinctive image in the minds of customers, investors, employees, etc., as compared to its competitors, while van Rekom (1997) explain that "corporate image always starts with an organization's corporate identity...managers concerned about the corporate image cannot ignore the organization's corporate identity". Finally, most writers (Holtzhausen and Fourie, 2008; Melewar, Bassett and Simoes, 2006; Melewar and Karaosmanoglu, 2006; Melewar and Bains, 2002; Bernstein, 2009; Melewar and Saunders, 1998; Markwick and Fill (1997)) agree that managing corporate identity represents an effective strategic tool to achieving a competitive advantage.

2.6 Employee Commitment: Why Bother?

Initially, corporate identity was understood as selling the vision of leadership and desired identity to external stakeholders, with top executives, marketing, purchasing, PR focusing on external stakeholders only. Indeed, Holtzhausen and Fourie (2008) revealed that companies spend large resources on managing and communicating their corporate identity to external audiences, and put less effort into communicating it to employees. In the past, this approach functioned well mainly due to there being only a few contacts between insiders (mainly employees) and outsiders (external stakeholders) (Hatch and Shultz, 1997). However, as Hatch and Shultz (1997) pointed out, networking, and the new focus on customer service increased the levels of interaction between organizational members and external audiences such as suppliers, customers, etc., combined with several roles undertaken by organizational members as "insiders"(i.e. as employees) and as "outsiders" (i.e. as consumers, community members or members of special interest groups). This meant that the focus on "selling" corporate identity to external audiences only had to shift to gaining both "outsiders" and "insiders" buy-in to the corporate identity. Harris and de Chernatony (2001) further confirmed the role of employees as brand "ambassadors" and the strong impact of these employees on how external stakeholders i.e. customers perceived the brand. Melewar and Karaosmanoglu (2006) explained that while management has control over the message they communicate to external audiences, **a large amount of uncontrolled communication** flows free, beyond their control. It is why Harris and de Chernatony (2001) urged leaders to pay attention to potential inconsistencies between the desired image and the image projected through employee behavior. Bronn, Simcic, Engell and Martinsen (2006) quoting McKinsley (2005) warned that "companies are what they are, not what their executives want them to be perceived as being". The impact of employees on corporate identity programs is confirmed by empirical studies, with Markwick and Fill (1997) finding that "cooperativeness of company staff" is perceived by customers as essential in their decision of "buying " into the brand image. Findings by Melewar and Karaosmanoglu (2006) further confirmed that employee behavior influences and is perceived as a reflection of corporate identity, and that "organizations will have a better image and gain more recognition if their employees are able to represent the organization's values to external audiences". Finally, de Chernatony and Cottam (2008), quoting participants in their study, concluded that "the brand is nothing more than what people decide to do...a brand is delivered by the people, people are the brand or manifestations of what becomes the brand...if you don't have people at the front line who in their blood operate in a way that you want to emote with that brand then you are completely wasting your time...".

2.7 Hospitality Industry: The Role of Employees

Gill (2008) explained that high levels of employee-customer interaction characterize the hospitality industry. Solnet (2006) quoting Kelley (1992) and Mattila and Enz (2002) also highlighted that quality of employee-customer interactions represents a key strategic competitive weapon for service organizations as customers most often perceive the organization based on service received from employees. Solnet (2006) takes his idea further and referencing Wiley and Brooks (2000), points out that when employees have a negative perception of the organization customer perceptions will be affected negatively. Finally, Kandampully (2006) concludes that quality of service elevates the image of organizations in the minds of customers, offering the most important and sustainable competitive advantage against similar organizations.

2.8 The Case Study

A SWOT analysis undertaken within a large hotel brand revealed as a weakness the brand image within US (outdated, family oriented rather than a business brand) and the age of the products vs. those of competitors. However, a worldwide re-branding exercise (new logo, refurbishment, new bathroom experience, new scents, new approach to service standards, etc.) was rolled over with the aim of repositioning the brand from traditional, comfortable, unpretentious and affordable to fresh, modern and contemporary, a brand that met the needs of both leisure and the less price-sensitive corporate market. This was preceded by extensive customer market research, employee surveys, consultations, etc., following a new, more modern and contemporary logo was chosen to replace the old logo, new values introduced to emphasize the ideal behaviors and values of the brand, and new slogans stressed the customer satisfaction focus. A new intranet, meetings between management and staff, social events celebrating the re-branding, speeches and visits by senior board members, training, "heroes" of the month/year awards celebrating on-brand behaviors, new recruitment policies and strategies are only few approaches activities meant to communicate and gain employee buy-in to the new values.

CHAPTER 3.
METHODOLOGY

3.1 Literature Research

The first step in identifying previous studies was drawing a list with keywords, including names of writers, which were then used to perform searches on online journals. Keywords or phrases included "identity", "corporate identity", "organizational identity", "image", "organizational image", "corporate culture", "culture", "Hatch", "Shultz", "Balmer", "Bernstein", etc. A series of journals and search engines were useful, however the most helpful articles were found in Emerald and Harvard Business Review. After reviewing a large number of articles, the relevant from the irrelevant were separated and a new search was undertaken using new keywords or phrases identified during this step. While making my way through the many relevant studies, other relevant articles and writers were identified. In addition, all references were read, new articles and writers identified, and the search/print/read/identify relevant literature step repeated. One book stood out as repeatedly being referenced in my research titled Wally Ollins's 1994 *Corporate Identity*. Finally, some MBA course books (*Marketing Management* by Kotler and Keller; *Strategy-Process, Content, Context* by De Wit and Myer; *Crafting and Executing Strategy* by Thomson/Strickland/Gamble and *The New Era of Management* by Daft) were revisited in search of new information.

To better understand the history of the brand, its old corporate identity, its re-branding and new corporate identity, the old and the new culture, etc., access was required to a serious database of journals specializing in the field of hospitality, this was available from the Institute of Hospitality. Beside the Institute of Hospitality database, search engines like Google helped in identifying information both on corporate identity and more general subjects. Finally, the intranet of the organization provided essential information on its corporate identity, values, ideal culture, etc.

3.2 Primary Method: Qualitative Research

3.2.0 Reasons for Choosing This Approach

The research used a qualitative method in the form of semi-structured interviews. Every interviewee was asked a set of both open and closed questions; however, the discussions were open, building upon any particularly interesting and relevant ideas that were introduced by participants. Throughout the interviews it became obvious that a quantitative approach would have never obtained the level of details and depth of information needed for the study of such a complex subject. The qualitative approach enabled me to confirm or follow up on thoughts, comments and ideas presented by participants whose body language also helped with identifying more sensitive issues/subjects and prompted changes in my behavior/approach.

3.2.1 Sample Selection

The sample consisted of 18 interviewees from two hotels owned by the same brand. The interviews focused on employees from departments that closely interacted with guests, as according to previous studies these employees have the highest impact on corporate identity, and its perception by external stakeholders. No anonymity requests have been made regarding the name of the brand, hotel owners, and hotel names. However, I decided on not disclosing the name of the brand as it is my belief that this study is relevant to all organizations, hence the focus must be on the ideas introduced rather than on the brand itself. Therefore, the large flagship London hotel was named Large Hotel, the smaller hotel was called Small Hotel and the departments within the hotel (i.e., front office, food, and beverage, etc.) were labeled as A, B, C, D, E and F. In addition, the hotel brand was named Brand, the company owning the two hotels is Company, the main competitor was named Competitor and other competitors were called Competitor 1, Competitor 2, etc.

Large Hotel Sample

Due to the type of operations, some of the main departments at Large Hotel are operationally split into different sub-departments. To better understand perceptions of corporate identity within these sub-departments, compare perceptions with the identity of whole departments and with corroborate identity of the brand/company, employees in some of these sub-departments have also been interviewed. Thus, some of the participants were employees from sub-departments A1, A2, A3, B1, B2, B3 and D. Even within these sub-departments, employees had different work patterns (i.e., night/day staff) characterized by lower/higher levels of interaction with guests or with colleagues. It is why employees from the same sub-department but with different work patterns in the sub-department A3 have also been interviewed. Finally, due to the type of operation, Large Hotel employed not only permanent employees but also staff provided by employment agencies. It is why besides hotel permanent staff two agency employees in sub-department A2 and department D have also been interviewed.

Small Hotel Sample

Due to its smaller size and different type of operation, Small Hotel operated differently from Large Hotel. The hotel was not using services of employment agencies. All employees were permanent full/part-time staff directly employed by the hotel. The hotel was organized within fewer sub-departments, as most employees were cross-trained to perform all tasks within the departments. Department F did not exist in this hotel. Finally, the sample consisted of a diverse set of employees from different departments, backgrounds, ages, lengths of service, etc.

3.2.2 Interview Questions

The semi-structured approach allowed for high degrees of freedom in expressing ideas and perceptions, while also maintaining the relevance of the conversation. Generally, revealing employee attitudes consisted of two steps. During the first step, the question focused on employee perceptions based on specific examples linked to the factors proposed to influence corporate identity (i.e., how do you think Competitor employees perceive Brand employees?). Finally, the second question focused on understanding how employee perceptions influenced their perception of corporate identity (i.e., and how does this make you feel? Or, how does it make you feel about the company?). When necessary, following or closed questions were used to clarify perceptions or opinions. Ollins's work (pg. 160: 1994) provided a good start in developing the questions, but most questions were relevant to the hypotheses and goals of the research. Particular attention was given to avoiding leading questions, and the questions were developed in a simple format to avoid confusions or ambiguities. A few drafts were written until a final one was developed. A pilot study consisting of three interviews in Large Hotel was conducted to test the final draft and as result, a few questions were re-formulated. Overall, the format of the interview consisted of six parts.

The first question collected information on participants (age, length of service, type of contract, nationality, etc.) and identified employees that worked for other Brand hotels in the UK and abroad. This was an important step as previous studies found different perceptions of corporate identity within employee subgroups. When employees that worked for other Brand hotels were identified, they provided valuable information regarding the impact of strategy, structure and national culture on corporate identity.

The second step consisted of questions 2, 3, 4, 5 and 6. Questions 2, 3 and 4 were all proposed by Ollins (pg. 160:1994) to reveal in-depth organization identity as perceived by employees, based on their experiences. Questions 5 and 6 concluded this step and focused on exploring perceptions held by employees with regards to the level of alignment between ideal and actual identities.

The third part focused on employee perceptions of how external stakeholders perceived the company. Here, open questions were asked to reveal the impact of corporate, organizational or bi-polar images and corporate reputation on corporate identity. This section included questions 7 to 9.

Question 10 focused on revealing employee perceptions of company leadership, and assessing the impact of management teams on employee perceptions of corporate identity.

Question 11 focused on revealing employee perceptions of corporate strategy and structure, the level of perceived congruency between the values and strategies of Brand and Company, and its impact on employee perceptions of corporate identity.

Finally, question 12 focused on personal values of employees, perceptions of alignment between values of Brand and Company vs. their values, and the impact on their perceptions of the corporate identity.

All interviews were recorded and transcribed before being analyzed.

3.3 Secondary Method: Communicated Identity of Brand

Similarly, to Kiriakidou and Millward (2000) and Gotsi, Adriopoulus, and Wilson (2008) a review was undertaken of official company documents, websites, intranet, press releases or interviews conducted by newspapers with top senior managers. This allowed for "the identification of basic corporate descriptors and values from the perspective of the official organization and the top management board", (Kiriakidou and Millward, 2000). Several main descriptors and values of Brand were identified: training, investment in employee development, employee involvement, a great place to work, profit, competition, efficiency, responsible business, long-term focus, customer satisfaction, quality, innovation, best in class service, trust, communication, teamwork, results, environmental awareness, equal opportunities. Together with the employee survey described below, the secondary research played an important part in the study of factors such as subcultures, management behavior, etc.

3.4 Secondary Data: The Employee Survey

The employee survey was a valuable source of information, complementing the primary research method. In conjunction with the ideal values and descriptors identified during the secondary research, the employee survey provided important information on the alignment between the ideal and actual identity, and employee perceptions within different sub-groups.

3.5 Analysis

An initial comparison of communicated values and descriptors vs. employee survey was carried out to assess the level of alignment between the actual and communicated identity, and the level of alignment between perceptions within different departments. The transcribed interviews were analyzed using a structured approach: read all interviews - identify the information relevant to one specific factor – analyze – conclusions – recommendations – reflections – re-start the process for the next factor. This was a lengthy process; however, I was determined to ensure that results were accurate and relevant.

CHAPTER 4.
CONCEPTS AND FINDINGS

4.0 Introduction

This chapter introduces and explains concepts and their impact on corporate identity as it was described by previous studies, and the findings of my study in relation to these studies.

4.1 Organizational Identity

Balmer and Greyser (2003) quoted by He and Balmer (2007) explained that while Lippincott and Margulies were considered the "parents" of corporate identity, Albert and Whetten were first to introduce the concept of organizational identity in 1985 as "what is central, enduring, and distinctive about an organization's character" [Albert and Whetten (1985) in He and Balmer (2007), Kiriakidou and Millward (2000), Hatch and Shultz (1997)]. More recent definitions by Kiriakidou and Millward (2000) present organizational identity as "the set of beliefs a member holds about the existing character of the organizations", while Hatch and Shultz (1997) define organizational identity as "what members perceive, feel and think about their organizations". However, Van Rekom (1997) believes that corporate identity messages in corporate philosophies or corporate bibles are more directed towards gaining the acceptance of external stakeholders than representing the actual identity of the company. Yet, as employees perceive corporate identity based on their experience of the company, their perceptions are based on images that sometimes contradict the corporate identity messages promoted by management to external stakeholders (Kiriakidou and Millward, 2000). This leads to what Kiriakidou and Millward (2000) called identity gaps, that is discrepancies between the "ideal, aspirational self" (Balmer, 2008) and the actual organizational identity as perceived by employees, with employees dissociating themselves from the externally driven corporate identity, which is interpreted as rhetoric rather than reality, unwillingness to support the organization/brand or even opposition towards it (Kiriakidou and Millward, 2000; van Rekom, 1997; de Chernattony and Cottam, 2008). And, as most studies [Kiriakidou and Millward (2000), de Chernattony and Cottam (2008), Wilkinson and Balmer (1996), Melewar and Karaosmanoglu (2006), Gotsi, Andriopoulos and Wilson (2008), Gotsi and Andriopoulos (2007)] found wide corporate-organizational gaps within organizations we can argue that an in-depth understanding of the relationship between corporate and organizational identity is essential.

Findings

The comparison of the values/descriptors used by Brand against the employee survey results revealed significant discrepancies between the communicated and organizational identity. For example, employees reported negative perceptions of corporate identity in areas such as commitment to environment, trust, professional development, and provided mixed feedback on communication, involvement, training, working environment, teamwork, etc. The interviews conducted at Small and Large Hotels further identified negative employee perceptions in terms of quality, services offered to guests, work-life balance of employees, quality of product, investment, equal opportunities, etc. One interviewee argued that "...they (the company) say a lot about a lot of stuff but they don't really go with what they say," while another employee concluded that "the company often over promotes itself...". Employees believed that discrepancies between corporate and organizational identity affected perceptions of the corporate identity by external stakeholders, as another employee explained that "...we are promising something that we can't give.... we work 12 hours a day because we have less staff...and it interferes with your mood, you're supposed to be smiling and be happy with the guest. But if you're not smiling and you're not happy on the inside it is hard to project it to the guests...and they can see you are not too happy, even when smiling..." Furthermore, the employee survey confirmed that employees perceived large gaps between departments in terms of living by the Brand values at Large Hotel. This indicates inconsistency in how corporate identities are projected by employees to external stakeholders.

Conclusion

The study found a wide corporate-organizational identity gap within Brand. The findings are in line with previous studies by Kiriakidou and Millward (2000), Gotsi, Adriopoulos, and Wilson (2008), etc., and confirm the existence of large corporate-organizational identity gaps within organizations. Employees who pointed to these gaps dismissed the corporate identity of Brand as "fake" or happening only in an "ideal world" which, based on their experience of the company did not exist. For this reason, most employees displayed different levels of commitment to live by the values of Brand, and on several occasions, employees stated that they would leave the organization. Therefore, the study confirms previous findings by de Chernattony and Cottam (2008), Kiriakidou and Millward (2000), etc., regarding the significant impact of corporate-organizational gaps on employee perceptions of corporate identity, and their commitment to live by and promote the brand to external stakeholders.

4.2 Sub-cultures

Melewar and Karaosmanoglu (2006) refer to Schein (1985) to explain that the unitary, "one corporate identity" perspective is based on assumptions that all organizational members perceive the organization the same and share the same loyalty and commitment to the organization. However, Cornelissen and Elving (2003) referred to Van Maanen (1991) to emphasize that "employees are subject to a complex set of identifications....at times resulting in differentiated sub-cultures", while Melewar and Karaosmanoglu (2006) saw the organization as an "amalgamation of subcultures" which made "the evolution of a unitary corporate culture virtually impossible". Employee identification with a group or another will influence their attitudes, behavior, and commitment (Solnet, 2006) and may lead to different levels of alignment between the values of each subculture/group and values communicated by brands [Balmer and Wilson (1998) in Gotsi, Andriopoulos and Wilson (2008)]. This idea is supported by Kiriakidou and Millward's (2000) findings that different departments within organizations they studied had different perceptions of actual vs. ideal identities. The findings of these studies were confirmed by my research.

Findings

Overall, the initial comparison step between the ideal values and descriptors communicated by Brand, and the results of the employee survey revealed that employees from different departments perceived differently the size of the corporate-organizational identity gap within Brand, and identified different levels of loyalty and commitment to the brand values. For example, in regards to commitment of the company to environment and community, the percentage of employees agreeing that the company was committed was: 81% in the food & beverage department, 72% in kitchen, 50% in Sales & Marketing, 58% in Rooms Division, 63% in Engineering, 100% in housekeeping and 81% in administration. Similarly, in the Living the Brand Values section, the percentage of employees who agreed that "We show we care" was: 78% in the food & beverage department, 72% in kitchen operations, 50% in Sales & Marketing, 67% in Rooms Division, 63% in Engineering, 93% in Housekeeping and 81% in administration.

Research by Harris and de Chernatony (2001) provided further insights into the aspects of subcultures influencing corporate identity. They proposed these factors as affecting the "perceptual congruity", that is alignment between the perceived and communicated identities:

4.2.1 Similarity of Employees

Similarity of brand employees is defined as similarity in terms of age, experience, education, team and organizations tenure, and functional background (Harris and de Chernatony, 2001). Harris and de Chernatony (2001) first refer to Bantel and Jackson (1989) and Murray (1989) to argue that teams formed by employees with dissimilar characteristics will most likely have different values and "exhibit greater conflict" and completed the idea by referring to Lichtenstein (1997) to argue that within heterogeneous teams communication, team integration and consensus building are generally poorer. By contrast, Harris and de Chernatony referred to Robbins (1991), Bantel and Jackson (1989) and Wagner (1984) to argue that team members with similar characteristics will most likely have similar experiences and perspectives, shared values and communicate better and easier. Finally, Harris and de Chernatony proposed "the greater the similarity of brand team members, the more congruent will be their perceptions about the nature of their brand".

Findings

Age

One executive manager from the 55-64 years old category at Small Hotels felt that "there are the older people that are faithful to the company, the youngster just doesn't care, and they let down the service and the customer care...". However, this argument was not confirmed by my findings. For example, there were three interviewees in the 45-64 years old section and while the above employee had very positive feedback towards the company, another employee had mixed feelings while the last employee had very negative feedback and wanted to leave Brand. Therefore, we can observe different levels of loyalty and commitment to the company within this age group. The analysis of employee views within the 25-34 years group revealed that employees held different perceptions of the organization. In this case, two employees within this age group had positive feedback about the benefits provided by Company while another employee provided less positive feedback, one employee had very positive feedback about the company while most employees provided mixed feedback. Finally, while employees within this age group provided mixed positive and negative feedback, their perceptions on areas of improvement differed as well: one employee focused on improved communication, another one on consistency, another one on quality, another one on personal development, etc.

Individuals within each age group displayed different levels of loyalty/commitment to the company, and different perceptions of its actual corporate identity. This lead me to conclude that due to individual age groups not holding unitary, shared perceptions and commitment to the company, the age of employees had no impact on how corporate identity was perceived and lived by. This contradicts the idea introduced by Harris and de Chernatony (2001) who included age in the definition of "similarity of brand team members" and argued that "the greater the similarity of team members [in this case age], the more congruent will be their perceptions of their brand". The discrepancies found between perceptions held by executive managers vs. junior employees within the 45-64 years old group indicates that formation of sub-cultures within the organization is also affected by employee status and position within the company.

Functional Background

At departmental level, employees perceived differently both the level of commitment to the brand and the size of the corporate-organizational identity gap. An analysis of the interview information provided by employees in sub-departments B1 and B2 also found different levels of alignment between the corporate and organizational identity, and perception of Brand. For example, at Large Hotel an employee in B1 sub-department expressed her disappointment regarding the large gap between the positive picture "sold" to her when joining the company and the actual reality discovered at the workplace. Another employee in sub-department B2 argued that the company "is a good place to work for, we always try to improve, always try to do something better". The analysis of interviews in sub-department B2 revealed different perceptions and levels of alignment between corporate and organizational identity at individual employee level. In this case we observed the positive feedback provided by one full-time employee. The other interviewee is an agency employee and felt there is "no communication with the employee, individual talk, I don't think they have any connection with each individual". The same situation was found in department A where the employee in A1 pointed to the company strategy of employing agency workers as the main challenge. In A2, the employee felt that the main problem within the three Brand hotels he worked for was "being treated like a number in the book", in A3 one employee (day shift) indicated the cost-cutting strategy as the main problem within the company while the second employee (night shift) stated that the company had to improve benefits, wages, "go with what they say" and consistency across brand.

Finally, from four employees that worked within the UK in two Brand hotels owned by Company, one felt there was a significant gap between the two individual hotels regarding the alignment between Brand's communicated and its actual identity. The other three employees felt there were no discrepancies between the hotels in terms of standards, employee commitment, quality, etc. However, from these three employees one had a very positive perception of Company while another employee had an opposite view. One senior manager in Small Hotel confirmed the findings of the employee survey at Large Hotel and the differences in employee perceptions between the two hotels. Thus, we can observe discrepant perceptions of corporate identity at a unit (hotel) level.

The findings were very surprising. Interviews in department A and B indicated low levels of congruency between perceptions both within the two departments, sub-departments but most even within the same sub-departments. These findings seem to contradict Harris and de Chernatony's

(1989) proposal that similarity in functional background increases congruency in employee perceptions of the brand identity.

Length of Service

Mixed attitudes towards the company were found within each "length of service" group studied however these attitudes were based on departmental culture and management, personal relationships with senior management, present actions taken by the company in terms of staffing, benefits, etc. For example, one employee within the 5-10 years group stated "when I first started I enjoyed it but then we were fully staffed. Now there seems there are more people that leave and are not being replaced...I think it changed, unfortunately, probably since the credit crunch...". Therefore, length of service did not cause the change of perception and satisfaction with the company but the global economic situation, cutbacks, etc. However, from another perspective, one department D employee from the up to 1-year group stated that length of service within his department lead to a strong culture reflected in resistance to change, "non-equal" treatment for new employees vs. long-serving staff, and therefore lack of alignment to the company values (i.e. the "non-equality" situation described by this employee contradicts the corporate identity of Brand, and its values).

The study found different perceptions of the corporate identity within the "length of service" groups. This indicates that length of service per se has no direct impact on how individual employees perceive the corporate identity. However, the situation changes when we look at similarity of individuals within a group, case in which length of service was found to have a strong impact on corporate identity. This is because over time within a group, individuals together for a long time can develop a strong culture reflected in resistance to change and lack of alignment to values of the company.

National Culture

The largest sample of employees from the same nationality consisted of six interviewees. We will call this sample X. Another sample of six interviewees included employees of different nationalities but from the same geographical region and similar cultures (i.e. Eastern Europe). We will call this sample Y. The differences between perceptions were significant. When asked about what the company had to improve on, most answers within sample X focused on staff levels, wages, benefits, recruitment of the right people and general working hours. Employees within sample Y felt that the company should improve communication, staff development, customer service, understand people more, continuous improvement, management training, mentality, consistency, "go with what they say". The discrepancies between the two sample groups are more obvious when analyzing sample Y's perceptions of what was good about the company against sample X's perception of what needed to be improved. In this case, sample Y employees felt that some of the positive things about the company were: "we have a lot of benefits", "they pay for your time", "great staff", "good place for the people". Therefore, while sample X employees felt that some areas and factors needed improvement, sample Y employees had positive attitudes and feedback towards the same factors and areas. Another employee stated that "...it depends on the culture...I think that in Mediterranean countries they act more unprofessional...". The same employee further explained that in her country recruitment was based on "who you know not on what you know" and on "being presentable...if you are not good at showing yourself it is more difficult" which was different within UK, where "if you are more experienced than you have more chances to get the job". As the employee did not work for Brand in her country, recommendations for further research will be made in the Reflections chapter.

The study found that employees from two national cultures/blocks of similar cultures and working for brand hotels owned by the same company in UK held different perceptions of the actual corporate identity of Brand. This leads me to conclude that national culture of employees affects their perception of the company and its corporate identity.

Conclusion

Several subcultures were found within Brand, with employees perceiving differently the alignment between the corporate and organizational identity, and also perceiving differently their level of commitment to the brand. The study confirmed findings by Melewar and Karaosmanoglu (2006) that organizations are an "amalgamation of subcultures" and thus the evolution of a unitary corporate identity is "virtually impossible". Indeed, organizations consist of a multitude of identities rather than the one ideal corporate identity.

4.2.2 Shared Values

A. Employee Personal Values vs. Brand Values

Harris and de Chernatony (2001) proposed that brands perform better when personal values of employees are aligned and compatible with their values. De Chernatony and Cottam (2008) refer to Griseri (1998) to conclude that when discrepancies between employees' personal values and brand values exist, employees experience tension and reduced commitment to behaviors that while consistent with brand values may contradict own personal values. This scenario leads, according to de Chernatony and Cottam (2008) to inconsistencies in employee behavior and/or inconsistency in perceptions of corporate identity by external stakeholders.

Findings

The study confirmed that alignment between personal and brand values affects the commitment of employees to the company. For example, one employee felt that his personal values blended well with the values of Brand and explained "it is really increasing my commitment, it makes me feel good that the company see me as an honest, carrying person and also the fact that the company employs these kinds of people...". Another employee took the idea further and stated that "it's fine...we are here for the same reasons...it makes me feel good because if you are both working towards the same thing then it makes it a lot easier, it makes it a more enjoyable workplace" while another employee concluded that personal values and brand values "should be the same, because... it will help the hotel to provide a better service and make more money".

Conclusion

Employees stated that the higher the congruency between their personal and Brand's values, the higher their commitment to Brand. Thus, the study confirmed the ideas put forward by Harris and Chernatony (2001).

B. Employee Personal Values vs. Organization's Values

Following the same rationale, Harris and de Chernatony (2001) proposed that brands perform better when employees' personal values are aligned and compatible with the values of organizations. This suggests that the brand and the organization are two **different** entities **i.e.** franchising agreements.

Findings

A large gap between the values of Brand vs. Company was found. One employee felt that while Company was focused mainly on money and profit, Brand was more interested in "the branding of the hotel ... obtaining the standards and the guest satisfaction scores, living the Brand standards ...rather than directly the money side of it...", while another employee argued that "Company's first priority will be revenue...they are trying to make as much money as possible out of it, whereas Brand wants to create a good brand, a good service, so they are looking for something completely different than what Company is looking for". The conflicting goals and values of Brand vs. Company left employees frustrated and confused as "you've got two different owners of the business that are both trying to achieve different things out of the property", while another employee concluded that this situation affected her commitment and loyalty to both Company and Brand.

Conclusion

Employees stated that misalignment between values of Brand vs. Company influenced negatively their commitment to Brand. Conversely, employees believed that alignment between the values of Brand vs. Company increased their commitment to "live" the brand. The findings confirmed theoretical ideas by Harris and Chernatony's (2001).

C. Brand's Values vs. Organization's Values

Harris and de Chernatony (2001) further proposed that brands perform better when values of the brands and organizations are congruent because shared, consistent values guide employees to adopt the desired behaviors and eliminate confusion.

Findings

The level of alignment between the values of employees vs. organization was found to influence employee commitment and perception of Brand. For example, one employee felt that if her values will blend in with Company's values "it would change your perception, you would feel more motivated, and you would feel happy to work here."

Conclusion

Employees stated that lack of alignment between personal values vs. Company values influenced negatively their perception of corporate identity. In contrast, employees believed that the more aligned their personal and Company values the more committed they were to Brand. The findings confirmed the theoretical proposals by Harris and Chernatony (2001).

4.3 Corporate Image

Markwick and Fill (1997) defined corporate image as "the totality of a stakeholders' perceptions of the way an organization presents itself, either deliberately (for example, through planned public relations activities) or accidentally (for example, through comments made by staff or media comment" while Bernstein quoted by Hatch and Shultz (1997) concludes that corporate image is "not what the company believes it to be, but the feelings and beliefs about the company that exists in the minds of its audiences". With this in mind, Holtzhausen and Fourie (2008) refer to Grunig (1992) to emphasize that when employees have a positive image of the company they are more committed to it. Similarly, Baker and Balmer (1997) referring to Balmer (1996) argue that a positive corporate image translates into loyalty and willingness to work for the organization. However, Moingeon and Ramanantsoa (1997) point out that the image held by employees with regards to the company company is an internal image, and argue that it should not be confused with the external corporate image. However, the same writers agree on the existence of a link between the internal and external corporate image; for example, they explain that when companies have a negative external image (i.e. the company is perceived as a polluter or as producing low-quality products) the external image will affect the internal image. This idea is further supported by Hatch and Shultz (1997) who conclude that the manner in which organizational members are perceived by customers, competitors and other external stakeholders can influence the organizational identity as employees mirror themselves in the comments.

Findings

The research produced surprising results in relation to the impact of corporate image on employee perceptions. From the total of eighteen interviewees, five felt that perceptions of Brand by media or guests influenced their perceptions of Brand, four had no opinion on this subject while nine employees stated that their perceptions of Brand are not being influenced by perceptions held by media and guests. In brief, 35.70% of employees with an opinion on the subject felt that corporate image influenced their perception of Brand. For example, one employee stated that if the company was perceived negatively" ...the way I think would change because that means that if they think it is not good I will also think, well, this company has a problem, that is why these people think like this...the way I think about Brand would change". The same employee perceived negatively the organizational identity, so the negative corporate image would have been confirmed by his experiences of the hotel. 64.30% of employees with an opinion on the subject felt that corporate image had no influence on their perceptions of Brand. Employees from this group stated that negative perceptions were not generally caused by Brand but by unrealistic expectations from guests, individual employees' attitudes, individual hotels, etc. One employee in this group concluded that "...it doesn't influence at all the way I think about Brand because I have my opinion and it does not matter what the media says".

However, an employee who worked for two Brand hotels owned by Company made one interesting comment. As he was happy with the current hotel, he was not affected by the negative perception his friends held about Brand in terms of quality. Yet, at the second hotel he pointed to a large corporate-organizational identity gap and argued that if this question was asked when he worked for this hotel, he would have probably felt that they were right, and he would have tried to change his employer. Moreover, another employee mentioned that his friends' positive image of Brand made him feel proud to work for Brand and he was committed to acting as a part-time marketer if he was happy at work. The data received from these two employees seems to indicate tentatively that, when linked to a positive organizational identity a negative corporate image will not influence employee's perception of the brand. However, a negative corporate image seems to bear a significant impact on the commitment and loyalty of employees to the organization when the corporate image is confirmed by a negative organizational identity. Finally, a positive corporate image linked to a positive organizational identity (i.e. "if I am happy at work") has the potential to increase commitment to the brand.

Conclusion

This research complements Moingeon and Ramanantsoa's (1997) proposal that a negative external image affects the internal image held by employees, and argues that most likely negative external images will only affect employees' perceptions when linked to a negative organizational identity, that is when employees believe that the negative image is confirmed by their own experiences of the company. This study complements previous proposals by Grunig (1992) in Holtzhausen and Fourie (2008) that a positive image of the company causes increased commitment to the company and argues that corporate image can have a significant impact on employee commitment, loyalty and perceptions of the company but only when linked to a positive organizational identity. We can conclude that while corporate image seems to affect employee perceptions and commitment, it is more likely that its impact is conditioned by employee perceptions of the organizational identity.

4.4 Organizational Image

Dutton and Dukerich (1991) are introduced by Balmer (2008) as "fathers" of the organizational image concept, which they later renamed as construed external image [Dutton (1994) in Balmer (2008)]. Dutton and Dukerich defined organizational image as "the way in which employees conceptualize how others see their corporation" (Balmer, 2008), while Balmer (2008) further explained the concept as representing employees' "beliefs about beliefs", their envisioned identity. Following their study of the New York Port Authority, Dutton and Dukerich (1991) quoted by Hatch and Shultz (1997) argued that there was a link between organizational identity and organizational image. Finally, Harris and de Chernatony (2001) argued that managers should encourage employees to provide feedback regarding their beliefs on how customers perceived them, as managers need to understand the differences in perceptions of the brand.

Findings

From the total of 18 employees only 9 employees did not work for Competitor or did not have friends working for Competitor, and therefore only 9 employees provided data on how they believed competitors perceived them, without being influenced by previous work experiences or feedback from their friends. 12.5% employees stated that how employees of Competitor perceived Brand employees influenced their perception of Brand. The other 87.5% employees, whom we will call the No group, generally felt that "it would be their opinion, while I would have mine". This idea seems further confirmed by an employee who believed that the perception of Competitor about Brand was positive and yet this did not change his perceptions or commitment to the company and its values, as he already knew the company was good. However, the link between the image and organizational identity, initially introduced in the section on corporate image seems to hold some influence on employees' perceptions. For example, one employee stated that competitors have a good perception of Brand and this made her feel good. However, when asked how this positive image affected her perception of Brand, she stated that "it is kind of fake, because everybody thinks this hotel has lots of challenges, you can learn different things, get a lot of training but actually we're not getting any of it. From outside, someone would think-because you work for this company you must have a great job, you are really happy, while most people working here, including myself would just think we are stuck in one place". This indicates that a positive organizational image contradicted by a negative perception of organizational identity may affect negatively employee perceptions of Brand.

Conclusion

Organizational image alone has little to no impact on how employees perceive corporate identity. However, a positive organizational image seems to affect employee perceptions of corporate identity in a negative way, when not supported by a positive organizational identity. This confirms the link between organizational image and organizational identity as proposed by Dutton and Dukerich (1991) in Hatch and Shultz (1997). There was not sufficient data to reach a more informed conclusion, which is why the organizational image-organizational identity link will be recommended for further research in the chapter on Reflections.

4.5 Bi-polar Identity

Balmer (2008) introduced the concept of bi-polar identities, defined it as "perspectives of the other...for instance, Airbus vis-à-vis Boeing, Oxford University vis-à-vis Cambridge University, etc..." and argued that different identities are contingent and relational. Balmer's description of bi-polar identities was rather short with no reference to the types of identities that are contingent and relational with bi-polar identities. Drawing on Balmer's (2008) belief that studying identity and identification is important given that perceptions can translate in behavior, impact of bi-polar views on employees' perceptions of Brand was also studied.

Findings

From nine employees with an opinion, seven felt that their perception of Brand as compared with other competitors such as Competitor, Competitor1, etc., did not influence their perceptions or commitment to Brand. Only two employees stated the contrary, but even in this case the body language and tone of voice of one employee indicated uncertainty regarding the answer.

Conclusion

A small number of employees within Brand indicated that bi-polar identities influenced their perceptions of Brand's corporate identity. We can argue that while bi-polar identities seem to have low potential to influence employee perceptions, the large size of the sample that disagreed indicates that bi-polar identities have no significant impact on corporate identity.

4.6 Corporate Reputation

Harris and de Chernatony (2001) quoting Fombrun and Rindova (1996) defined corporate reputation as "a collective representation of a brand's past actions and results that describes brand's ability to deliver valued outcomes to multiple stakeholders". Balmer and Grey (2000) argued that a favorable reputation plays a major role in attracting high caliber employees, employees who play a crucial role in communicating the corporate identity to external audiences. Solnet (2006) underlined the impact of external prestige of an organization, therefore reputation, on employee identification with the organization. Finally, Baker and Balmer (1997) refer to Balmer's (1996) model of corporate identity formation to argue that a favorable reputation translates in increased loyalty to the organization from all stakeholders, including employees.

Findings

Corporate reputation has a significant impact on decisions of the employees joining a company. These employees stated that before joining the company "I heard only very good things about it (Brand). It was just as famous as Competitor", "it is a very big company....everybody knows it...it is a name you know, a good name", "a great company to work for...I thought it will be a big advantage to work here", "the biggest company" while another employee concluded that "I was thinking that it is not possible to join in such a big chain and I was scared because I was thinking that I will not be enough for this company". Within this sample, one employee joined Brand from Competitor and throughout the duration of the study, three employees were promoted as Supervisors within their departments, two completed their NVQ in Hospitality, one employee started her second NVQ, and another employee started his first NVQ and was training as Supervisor. However, after the initial exuberance created by the corporate reputation of Brand, one employee experienced a "culture shock" due to the large gap between her expectations based on the reputation of Brand, the corporate identity communicated during her induction and the actual, experienced organizational identity. This employee mentioned that given this large gap, she lacked motivation "to do anything" and left the company on several occasions. We notice again the link between a positive reputation –negative organizational identity and its negative impact on employee perceptions.

One particularly interesting idea surfaced based on perceptions held by two employees. When these employees were asked to compare Brand with Competitor, they felt that the comparison was inadequate because Brand had a four-star rating while Competitor had a five-star rating. As one employee explained: "I am going by Competitor's reputation...I associate Competitor with luxury, its previous history, its past reputation...it's like you would try to compare a car (Competitor) with a motorbike (Brand): different chains, different star ratings...". Furthermore, this employee felt that his perception of Brand is not being influenced by bi-polar views of Brand vs. Competitor because Competitor was a five-star chain and it was normal to be better than Brand who had a four-star rating. However, as we recall Balmer (2008) explained that Hilton held two different identities: one in the UK and one in the USA. A very similar situation applies in Competitor's case, a fact confirmed by the researcher who has previously worked in a senior management position for Competitor UK and confirms that within the UK, most Competitor hotels are of a four-star rating rather than the five stars rating assumed by the two employees. This idea raises several questions that could represent the object of future research, and this will be further discussed in the chapters on Conclusions and Reflections.

Conclusion

A positive corporate reputation plays a major role in attracting high performing, committed employees, provided that the actions of the company met their expectations (i.e promotion, investment in personal development). These findings are in line with proposals by Balmer and Gre (2000) that a favorable reputation is crucial o attracting high performing employees.

The study also complements proposals by Solnet (2006) and Balmer (1996) in Baker and Balmer's (1997) that a favorable reputation increases employee loyalty and identification with the organization. It is also concluded that a favorable reputation affects employee commitment and identification with the organization only when linked to a perceived positive organizational identity. When corporate reputation is not supported by a positive organizational identity, the study found that a positive reputation affects negatively employee perceptions and commitment to Brand.

4.7 Corporate Structure

Melewar and Saunders (1998) referred to Chajet (1989), Olins (1986) and Strong (1990) to emphasize the important impact of corporate structure on corporate identity. Melewar and Saunders identified centralization and decentralization as two factors that are leading to companies in each country developing own identities. Balmer (2008) points out that brands can have "a life their own of its own", that is one brand can have separate identities than the institution or nation they evolved from. Balmer provides the example of franchising agreements by referring to the Hilton brand, which had two identities, one in the UK and one in the USA. However, Cornelissen and Elving

(2003) argue that "the construct of structure (e.g. division, geographic, hybrid, etc.) per se is not of a direct and immediate effect on corporate identity...". In this context, Cornelissen and Elving explain that within large organizations senior managers can decide both how divisions and the corporate group are managed, and how they are presented to the outside world. However, Cornelissen and Elving (2003) admitted there is little empirical evidence to support these claims.

Findings

Both employees who worked each in two Brand hotels owned by different companies (franchised properties) pointed to large gaps between the corporate identity of Brand and its actual identity as experienced within Company. For example, one employee stated that "I was working for Brand hotel in Slough, it was not a Brand-owned hotel, it was a franchise so...I think they have to improve standards in franchised properties. For example, the owner in Slough was taking shortcuts, cutting costs against quality...the name was Brand, but the standards were not Brand. And the staff was not at all happy, they did not feel part of Brand, because they don't get all the benefits, all the development, they were not even being told about all these things...". As standards were different and employees did not identify with Brand, we can observe that at Brand Slough hotel, the perceived corporate identity differed from the corporate identity of Brand. When investigating within an international context, the findings were mixed, mainly because only two employees worked **previously** for Brand hotels both in the UK and abroad. One employee perceived no discrepancies between the UK and the two hotels he worked for abroad, while the other employee felt that the hotel abroad had better standards due to lower staff turnover. However, employees from different national cultures perceived corporate identity of Brand within the UK differently. But the differences in management style and actions within the UK did not seem to have led to increased alignment in terms of perceptions between UK nationals (sample X) and the other sample of foreign nationals

(Sample Y). This contradicts Cornelissen and Elving's (2003) statements that corporate structure had no direct influence on corporate identity.

Conclusion

Corporate structure, in this case, the franchised, decentralized structure of Brand was found to affect corporate identity, as different companies owning Brand hotels within and outside the UK developed a multitude of corporate identities rather than the unique, ideal corporate identity promoted by Brand. This confirms findings by Melewar and Saunders (1998) that corporate structure has a significant impact on corporate identity.

4.8 Corporate Strategy

Melewar and Karaosmanoglu (2006) underline the important impact of corporate strategy on corporate identity, particularly in cases of programs that involve changes to corporate identity. Melewar and Karaosmanoglu found that employees within organizations they studied stated that corporate strategies impacted their perceptions and commitment to new corporate identities, especially in cases of re-structuring a workforce. Many companies focus nowadays on short-term financial performance and targets, and this may lead to "brand destroying strategies", which affects brand culture negatively (de Chernatony and Cottam, 2008). From another perspective, Hernstein, Mitki, and Jaffe (2007) referred to Miles and Mangold (2004) to emphasize that human resource strategies also play a crucial part in managing the corporate identity successfully. Finally, Melewar and Karaosmanoglu (2006) conclude, "in other words, corporate strategy determines what a company's identity is and is going to be".

Findings

The growth strategy, franchising in this case, affected the perception of the ideal corporate identity. One employee noticed discrepancies within franchised properties i.e. employee development and benefits, or how guests experienced the brand and concluded, "...as a company, if you want to grow as a franchise you must have the same standards". Employees felt frustrated and confused by conflicting strategies of Brand and Company, and by their different goals (brand image vs. profit). The cost-cutting strategy adopted by Company was a primary reason for employees perceiving wide corporate-organizational gaps within Company and based on these perceptions, employees stated that both their perceptions of Brand values and guests' perception of the corporate identity were affected. For example, one employee noticed that "I think the company behaves more on money, it wants to get as much money as possible despite it causing a problem elsewhere...isn't that the Your Stay, Your way? ...It can't really be Your Stay, Your Way if there are not enough people to fulfill everything you want, so if you want your room cleaned every day from top to bottom, you don't have the staff to do that, or if you want extra pillows, there is not enough staff to carry it up and back in the time you want it, or room service...there is only one person and he has 20 covers, of course they are not going to get it in time, so really, Your Stay Your Way is about what they want in the time they want and there is not enough people to do that ". The same employee concluded that the cost-cutting strategy translated in overworked, tired, unhappy employees visibly affecting the way employees projected the corporate identity to guests. Linked to the cost-cutting strategy, Large Hotel employed agency employees, which offered them flexibility in terms of cost-control. However, several full-time employees noticed that agency employees lack commitment to the company as "they don't want to stay here, they just come, get the money and that is it", "the agency come here just to work and that's it...they come here just a day or two...", an idea confirmed by an agency worker as well who stated that "I don't know that much about Brand, I just come here to work and go home...all I need from this hotel is money". From another perspective, when asked if he felt he had the same career opportunities and benefits as permanent employees, an agency employee felt he had fewer benefits and career opportunities, and this affected his perception of the company and its communicated identity. Both agency employees confirmed the lack of training and knowledge in terms of the culture, values and operational procedures of the company. Besides the recruitment of agencies, two other permanent employees felt that one of the biggest problems both at Large and at Small Hotel was the recruiting strategy, that is employing the wrong staff which in their opinion resulted in lack of commitment to expected behaviors of Brand.

Conclusion

First, the growth strategy chosen by Brand had a significant impact on how the unitary, ideal corporate identity was adhered to across the brand with employees perceiving, living by and projecting a multitude of corporate identities rather than a unitary corporate identity. Second, cost-cutting and restructuring strategies employed by Company to achieve profit targets were perceived by employees as conflicting with the corporate identity of Brand (i.e., quality, care for employees, guest satisfaction, etc.) and resulted in employees rejecting the corporate identity claims of Brand. This study further confirms findings by Melewar and Karosmanglu (2006) and de Chernatony and Cottam (2008) that short-term financial-oriented strategies such as re-structuring the workforce have a high probability of transforming in "brand destroying strategies" and affect negatively the brand supporting culture. Employing agency workers in order to control costs was one such brand-destroying strategy. The study also confirms findings by Miles and Mangold (2004) in Hernstein, Mitki, and Jaffe (2007) with regards to the crucial impact of recruitment strategies on managing corporate identity.

4.9 Leadership

Hatch and Shultz (1997) argued that actions and behaviors of top managers influence the organizational identity, as managers represent themselves a symbol of the corporate identity they communicate. Similarly, de Chernatony and Cottam (2008) refered to Chatman and Cha (2003) to conclude "the example set by leaders carries more weight with employees than codified policy statements". The idea is supported by studies by Melewar and Karaosmanoglu (2006) who found that leadership was perceived as a crucial factor in setting up standards for employee behavior, as employees perceived managers as role models. However, Johnson (2008) argues that many managers "communicate rhetoric...but fail to embrace the practices outlined in their rhetoric themselves" and concludes that employees "won't do as you (the manager) say, but they often will do as you do".

Findings

A few relevant findings of the employee survey are presented below, revealing the percentage of employees agreeing with the statement from "Statement" column.

Statement	F&b	Kitchen	Sales/marketing	Rooms	Engineering	Housekeeping	Administration
My Manager lives the Brand Values	70%	83%	50%	91%	63%	93%	90%
My Manager sets a good example for me	78%	89%	58%	91%	63%	100%	100%
The Management Team sets a good example for all of us	70%	78%	42%	79%	63%	93%	90%
WE live the Brand Values	76%	71%	63%	70%	54%	83%	80%

It can be observed that within the departments of Large Hotel, employees perceived different levels of management commitment and personal example in living by the values of Brand, with some managers adopting the brand values more than other managers. However most employees agreed that leadership teams affected their own behavior and commitment to live by Brand's values. One employee explained that when managers did not adhere to the Brand values he felt that "...these managers are seniors to yourself so it does not make you want to achieve lot more...if they are your seniors and do not put any effort in, you look at them and say: Well, I don't need to either". Another employee stated that managers had to live by the values of Brand as "...you (the manager) lead by example...if you're not living the brand, the staff will see that and will pick up on that...if your managers don't do it, then why should we bother to do it?" Overall, employees unanimously agreed on the impact of leadership teams on their behavior and perception of Brand.

Conclusion

The study confirms previous proposals by Hatch and Shultz (1997), Johnson (2008), etc., and findings by Melewar and Karaosmanoglu (2006) with regards to the big impact of management behavior on employee perceptions, and on the adoption of Brand values.

Discussion

Having worked within and managed hotels for half of my life, I felt unease with the conclusion that Leadership and Management are attributed such a large impact on the success or failure of corporate identity. Throughout my career, I have worked with or managed a large variety of people placed at all levels within the leadership hierarchy. If you ever worked in hospitality, you will acknowledge the existence of far too many leaders whose incompetence, lack of vision and inability to lead are "compensated" by an ability to talk the talk throughout the ranks. As you go down the ranks, a large number of employees are working hard to compensate for the inability of their leaders to well...lead. So, at this point, you may ask yourself: "why were you so uneasy with the conclusion that leadership represented a top factor in the corporate identity context?" Employees are too quick to placing fault on the leader. In my experience, the leader represents a symptom, an effect rather than a cause. Undoubtedly, leaders and managers have a big impact on corporate identity, but they do so because they may. A culture based on meritocracy and achievement will quickly weed off inefficient leaders, just as it will weed off any other employee whose values lack congruence with the high-performance values of the company. As Jack Welch (143: 2005) once said, these people are "change killers, cut them off early". (If I remember correctly, he emphatically called them "poison"). Briefly, in a culture of meritocracy, the company will go to extreme efforts and put the best mechanisms in place to ensure that the right people are brought on board, and occasionally quickly "cut off early" when the wrong people slipped through the net. Given the importance of bringing the right people on board, I found this first piece of research insufficient to assessing the quality of recruitment practices and its impact on corporate identity. Hence, I decided on carrying out a different study, which investigated the efficiency of recruitment practices with a twist. **It is my belief that** bringing the right people on board is the one action that most companies struggle with, and this is often reflected in inconsistencies between the many types of brand identities I introduced throughout this study.

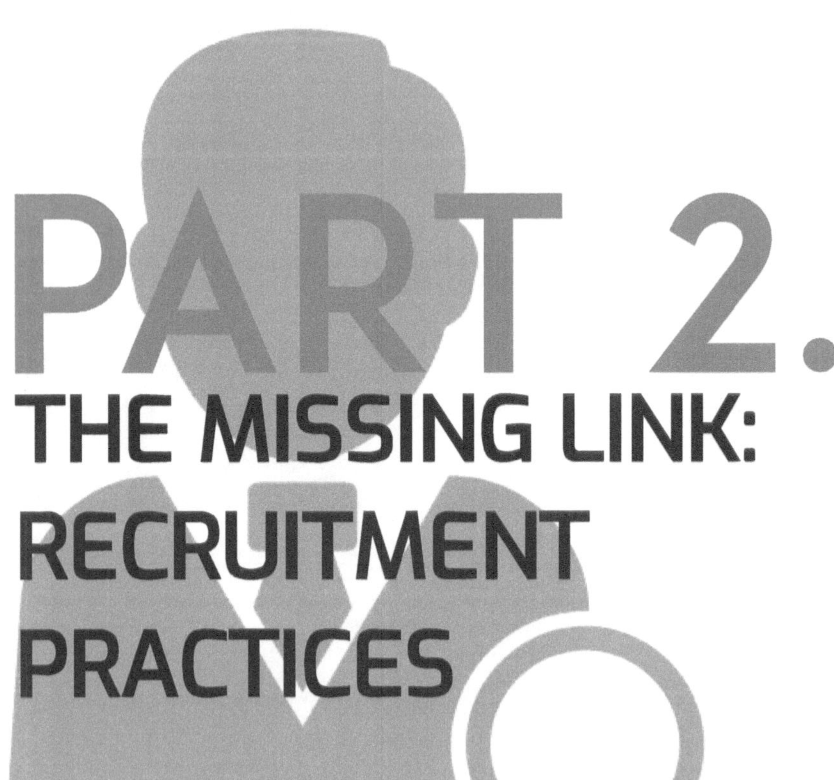

PART 2.
THE MISSING LINK: RECRUITMENT PRACTICES

CHAPTER 1.
ABOUT THE STUDY

This study investigated the extent to which managers and HR professionals consider corporate identity when recruiting the right "brand people", and the efficiency of recruitment practices. The sample consisted of 14 managers with recruitment responsibilities in four hotels within Brand, and a quantitative method was employed (online survey including closed and open questions). I am not aware of previous studies on the subject, hence the research is exploratory, and meant to "open doors" to further research.

Previous studies were reviewed prior to developing a questionnaire meant to assess the efficiency of recruitment practices vs. findings within the social psychology field. The survey was sent to managers in four hotels of Brand and the results were compiled in tables that allowed for easy analysis (i.e., percentages). Previous research was reviewed to determine the relationships between corporate identity, employees' perceptions and corporate image.

First, the study found that managers considered mainly operational aspects when recruiting employees, matching specific skills to job roles, as opposed to matching character and values to brand values, as advocated by most management academics.

Second, previous studies emphasized the importance of people in hospitality, given the high levels of employee-customer interaction. All managers surveyed acknowledged this aspect.

Finally, the study found that managers are overwhelmingly unaware of scientific findings on factors that may affect recruitment decisions they made. Overall, it was found that recruitment practices are inefficient, and managers are likely to bring on board people who not necessarily match the values of Brand.

The study was highly beneficial and identified recruitment as the primary factor affecting corporate identity. This suggests that management teams represent an effect of inefficient recruitment practices, rather than a cause of internal marketing failures. Finally, recruitment must be incorporated into the marketing function, and scientific findings must be incorporated within recruitment practices. In doing so, organizations will maximize the impact of their recruitment decisions, bring the right people on board, and ultimately deliver a consistent corporate identity.

CHAPTER 2.
INTRODUCTION

2.0 Background of Research

While studying for my MBA I became very interested in corporate identity and the factors affecting its success. Most academics acknowledge the impact of employees on corporate identity, and on corporate image (perceptions of brands held by external stakeholders i.e. customers). And, management teams are mentioned most often as a primary cause to discrepancies between corporate identity messages, employee perceptions, their commitment to live by the brand values and actual perceptions held by customers. However, in the case of Brand, the company and management went to great lengths to communicate, promote and get buy-in from employees. And yet, the internal marketing program of Brand failed to achieve consistency between the promoted identity and actual perceptions. It is why the idea that leadership alone represented the main cause of identity gaps required more investigation. Specifically, the recruitment process was identified by many previous studies as a primary pillar to successful companies, and to their corporate image (Collins, 2001; Pink, 2009; Hallier and Leopold, 1996). Hence, if recruitment is of such importance, one may ask a very obvious question: are managers equipped with the knowledge and skills required to recruiting the right employees and brand people, including recruitment of management and leadership teams? Could it be that the root cause to these identity gaps may not necessarily be managers per se, but the recruitment practices that led to recruiting employees (including managers) in the first place? I decided on another approach to studying this matter and turned my attention to scientific and psychology literature for a more in-depth understanding of human biases that affected and hijacked the recruitment decisions made by management teams and HR professionals.

2.1 Case Study

The study was conducted within Brand. As discussed, Brand went through a worldwide re-launch, with the goal of repositioning itself as contemporary, fresh and relevant. However, one year after re-launching, research carried out as part of my MBA programme found large gaps between the corporate and organizational identity of Brand. Throughout the study employees singled out management teams and leadership as the primary cause affecting their perceptions of Brand. This confirmed previous findings (Hatch and Shultz, 1997; Melewar and Karaosmanoglu, 2006; Johnson, 2008; de Chernatony and Cottam, 2008). In a first instance, previous studies were reviewed, and identified gaps in recruitment practices between traditional management practices and findings within the field of psychology. A survey was developed to explore perceptions and practices of management teams in relation to various psychological biases in recruitment. The study encourages companies to re-consider the allocation of resources, and focus on employing the right employees vs. tackling the effect of inefficient recruitment decisions.

2.2 Aims and Objectives

2.2.1 Aims of Research

The research assessed the impact of recruitment practices on corporate identity and the extent to which corporate identity is being considered when recruiting employees. The study also investigated the efficiency of recruitment practices, the levels of knowledge on/and practical use of scientific findings in recruiting Brand employees. Finally, the research provides recommendations to support organizations in bringing the right people on board, align corporate messages to the guest experiences and ultimately deliver a consistent corporate image.

2.2.2 Objectives of Research

a. Asses the extent to which corporate image is being considered by management and HR professionals when recruiting Brand employees.

b. Evaluate the contribution of employees to corporate image.

c. Examine the effectiveness of the recruitment process in relation to corporate image.

d. Provide recommendations for improvement.

2.2.3 Exploratory Questions

a. Is recruitment considered a Human Resources or a Marketing function?

b. What is the role of employees in relation to corporate identity and corporate image?

c. Are recruiters and managers equipped with the skills required to bring the right people on board?

CHAPTER 3.
METHODOLOGY

3.0 Introduction

This study further assesses the relationship between corporate identity, organizational identity, and corporate image within Brand. We discussed about the impact of marketing to positioning brands, and stressed that corporate messages are noise unless experienced by stakeholders in day to day interactions with the brand. As such, it is rather important that employees live up to what the brand stands for. However, employees have personals values that are not always in sync with the brands they represent, which is why bringing the right employees on board is essential. In a nutshell, recruit the right people and good things will follow. This chapter will discuss the research approach, strategy and design, data collection, methods of analysis and ethical issues.

3.1 Research Design

Exploratory research is best used when there is a lack of or insufficient information and studies on a subject, with researchers looking to develop an idea and guidance from potentially a few participants. Generally, the method is unstructured, allows high levels of flexibility and includes qualitative information. I am not aware of previous studies on recruitment and marketing that approach corporate identity from this perspective. Hence, a case study on a relatively small sample of four hotels cannot provide a definitive answer to the questions I am addressing. However, this study develops an idea, brings arguments supported by theory and "opens doors" to further research. Hence, the research is exploratory, prompting further needs for research.

3.2 Approach to Research

3.2.0 Secondary Research

Qualitative and quantitative data was collected from previous studies and data readily available about Brand. Role of employees was thoroughly documented by previous studies exploring the concepts of corporate identity, organizational identity, and corporate image. Surveys on customer and employee satisfaction within Brand were already available (hence the quantitative approach), and used to both identify corporate identity vs. organizational identity and corporate identity vs. corporate image gaps within Brand. The study described in Part 1 (interviews) confirmed the identity gaps found within Brand.

3.2.1 Primary Research

3.2.1.1 Method Used

Semi-structured questionnaires were sent to managers within four hotels of Brand. The questionnaire method achieved its purpose better than a traditional qualitative approach (i.e., interview), by removing inhibition and restraint in providing information. This may not have been the case if an interview method was employed, given my position as an executive manager within the company.

3.2.1.2 Quantitative Method

Participants received a set of questions. Quantitative info was collected via closed questions (i.e., asking participants to rate their agreement with a statement), which allowed for data to be compiled in tables with numbers and percentages. With regards to some "open text" questions, participants were instructed to answer using the following format: record answer (yes/no/maybe/not sure) and explain the reasons for the answer, which was then compiled into table of responses. The study benefited from this approach by gaining an understanding of the amount of knowledge held by managers in relation to psychological biases in recruitment.

3.2.1.3 Qualitative Method

Qualitative data was collected via open questions. Text boxes enabled participants to explain their choices, record perceptions or identify new lines of thinking not thought to by the researcher. All closed questions included an "Other" text box enabling managers to record any thoughts, explain or identify new lines of thinking. Finally, all managers were instructed to fill in some open text questions by recording their answers (yes/no/maybe/not sure) and record the reasons for their answers. This method was highly beneficial as it clarified the reasons behind the perceptions held by managers vs. scientific findings, and it improved accuracy of quantitative results. For example, many managers thought that attractiveness of candidates affected recruitment decisions from a stereotyped viewpoint (i.e., attractive employees consciously recruited for airlines) but showed no awareness of own biases in the explanation provided. **In this case,** when a yes was recorded in the text box (managers acknowledged this factor as influencing recruitment), the answer was recorded as a "no" as managers did not acknowledge own biases. Finally, this method led me to identifying ideas I have not been considering by that time.

3.2.2 Sample Selection

The sample consisted of 11 participants, within four Brand hotels. Three other Brand ex-employees participated in the survey, taking the number of participants to fourteen. The survey focused on assessing managers' awareness of scientific findings with regards to biases in recruitment. Participants were all managers with recruitment responsibilities. No anonymity requests have been made with regards to the name of Brand, hotels owners, or hotel names. Regardless, I changed all the names, as this study is relevant to all similar organizations - the focus must be on the ideas discussed rather than on Brand.

3.2.3 Survey Questions

The semi-structured approach allowed high degrees of freedom in expressing ideas and perceptions, while closed questions (i.e., ratings) maintained focus and the relevance of the survey. Leading questions were avoided, and the questions presented in simple format avoiding confusions or ambiguities. All questions explored perceptions based on scientific findings on the human biases affecting decisions on recruitment. One limitation of the survey was that on a couple questions (i.e., impact of candidates' attractiveness) managers were asked for their thoughts, and self-reported their opinions. While the traditional self-reporting method is widely adopted in many management studies, given the many human biases uncovered throughout the study, it is safe to conclude that experiments will determine actual behavior better than self-reported methods.

3.3 Analysis

Survey questions and answers were organized in tables allowing for easy analysis of patterns. A structured approach was employed: read all answers – review information in text boxes – analyze – conclusions – recommendations – reflections – re-start the process for the next factor. This was a lengthy process, however it was important that results were accurate and relevant.

CHAPTER 4.
WHAT AFFECTS EMPLOYEE COMMITMENT?

4.0 Introduction

With small exceptions, previous studies pointed to leadership as a primary factor in affecting corporate and organizational identities, as leadership behavior carries more weight with employees than corporate statements [Hatch and Shultz, (1997); Chatman and Cha (2003) in Chernatony and Cottam (2008), Melewar and Karaosmanoglu (2006)]. Indeed, Johnson (2008) ironically concludes that many managers and leaders "communicate rhetoric...but fail to embrace the practices outlined in their rhetoric themselves" and concludes that employees "won't do as you (the manager) say, but they often will do as you do".

4.1 Leadership: Effect or Cause?

Collins (11:2001) found that in reality, "great companies paid scant attention to managing change, motivating people or creating alignment". Great companies focused on a "First Who...Then What" concept, that is they "first got the right people on the bus, the wrong people off the bus and the right people in the right seats – and then they figured out where to drive it", and "they hired self-disciplined people who didn't need to be managed, and then managed the system, not the people" (Collins, 125:2001). Moreover, Collins (74:2001) found that "expending energy trying to motivate people is largely a waste of time...if you have the right people on the bus they will be self-motivated". However, bringing the right people on the bus is difficult in service organizations. As Frei and Moriss (93:2012) brilliantly argued, "In an ideal world, all of your employees would be high in attitude and high in aptitude. They are highly motivated dream-team employees who are also deliciously competent...the problem is you're not the only one who wants these people, and as a result they're expensive" (Frei and Moriss, 94:2012). Instead, in line with findings by Collins, Frei and Moriss explain that as most service organizations cannot afford to pay high wages to all employees, it was essential that the right people with the right characteristics were recruited through a very rigorous process, followed up with their development (Frei and Moriss, 92-96:2012). And just as Collins, Frei, and Moriss found that organizations they studied "...try to weed out misfits early in the investment...anyone who's uncomfortable with these values or the way they manifest in his or her job is encouraged to leave during the training stage. Strongly encouraged." (Frei and Moriss, 96-97:2012).

It is therefore important to observe that these studies found management functions such as motivating people as secondary to" bringing the right people on the bus". As Collins and Frei and Moriss emphasized, the focus in great companies was not on management behavior per se, but on recruiting the right people and offloading the wrong people off the bus at all levels. To conclude the idea, De Chernatony and Cottam (2008) and several writers quoted by Hallier and Leopold (1996) suggested that the initial recruitment process was crucial to the success of organizations. If the right people are recruited and socialized, the organization is able to build-in long-term employee satisfaction and meet the flexible needs of the business (Hallier and Leopold, 1996). Hence, recruitment of the "right people" rather than management behavior represents the main factor to be reviewed by Brands if they are to build a strong corporate identity and image. Or, as Collins (44:2001) concludes: "...the point is the degree of sheer rigor needed in people decisions in order to take a company from good to great". In this context, management behavior represents a symptom of recruitment practices rather than a cause of inconsistencies within the corporate identity and image.

4.2 Human Biases in Recruitment

The most often used method of recruiting employees is interviewing candidates. However, as Nobel winner psychologist Daniel Kahneman pointed out (225:2011), "conducting an interview is likely to diminish the accuracy of the selection procedure...because interviewers are overconfident in their intuitions, they will assign too much weight to their personal impressions..."And Hood (36, 83: 2009) concludes that "for making choices, most of us feel confident that we evaluate the evidence objectively, weight pros and cons and act according to reason...when we decide there are all sorts of biases operating that are independent of reason. We don't necessarily have the free will to choose". Finally, research and experiments by Wiseman (43-44:2009) found that while employers believe they chose candidates with the best qualifications and personal skills for the job, in reality, "interviewers are often deluding themselves about how they make up their minds and in reality, they are unconsciously swayed by a mysterious and powerful force". And Kahneman (97:2011) further explains "you have intuitive feelings and opinions about almost everything that comes your way. You like or dislike people long before you know much about them. You trust or distrust without knowing why..." and "we are confident when the story we tell ourselves comes easily to mind...and will achieve high confidence much too easily by ignoring what it does not know" (Kahneman, 239:2011).

So, what biases are we talking about?

4.2.1 Gender of Recruiter

Trivers (254:2011) quotes several studies by Bloise and Johnson (2007), Singer (2006) or Williams and Matingley (2006) to conclude that "... men are likely to be less compassionate toward others than are women. They are less likely to read emotions correctly from facial expressions, less likely to remember emotional information…and much less likely than women to show compassion towards others…"

Findings

42.86% of respondents stated that this factor had no impact on recruitment decisions, uncovering a gap between management perceptions/awareness and findings in psychology. Moreover, managers who agreed on the influence of these factors showed no awareness of what these biases were and how they affected decisions. One manager, for example, stated that "birds of a feather flock together (like attracts like)", another manager mentioned that "it depends on the job role…some people may prefer a certain sex…" referring, therefore, more to stereotypes about candidates rather to their own gender bias as recruiters.

4.2.2 Positivity Bias

Trivers (134:2011) referred to different experiments that measured people's unconscious implicit biases to show that people generally prefer young to old age, associating young with positive features. However, starting with the age of 40 people's explicit bias (what we say we care about) declines. This means that as they grow older, people of that age group advocate that "older is better" although studies found they still implicitly associate youth with positive features. Trivers concludes, "…the positivity effect requires no suppression of negative information or affect. The bias occurs right away. People simply do not attend to the negative information, do not look at it, and do not remember it". Hence, age of the interviewer may affect his perception of older or younger candidates.

Findings

Fifty percent of respondents stated that age of interviewers affected recruitment decisions "but it shouldn't", in line with previous findings with the psychology field. However, there is no awareness with regards to the workings exerted by this factor on employment decisions. For example, one manager explained that "younger interviewers can have a lack of experience which combined with overconfidence can lead to wrong decisions".

4.2.3 Willpower

Kahneman (225:2011) referred to a study of parole officers to conclude "the prospects of a convict being granted parole changed significantly during the time that elapsed between successive food breaks in the parole judges' schedules". Psychologists like Roy Baumeister demonstrated repeatedly that willpower is not a fixed trait, but works like any another muscle. Baumeister noticed that the more effort we put into performing mental tasks, the more tired we become, and the more control we delegate to the automatic but highly-biased automatic decision-making system (i.e., intuition). Labeled as ego depletion, this effect has two ramifications: first, our willpower is being diminished, and second, our cravings increase. Stress depletes willpower, and with it our ability to control our emotions, behaviors, and cravings. (Baumeister & Tierney, 2012) When we have low reserves of willpower we become "cognition misers," often deciding with little deliberation; we compare less, "satisfice" more, and focus on one feature of products, e.g., the cheapest, the best, the most available, and so forth. (Baumeister & Tierney, 2012) Jonathan Levav beautifully demonstrated this effect in several experiments. In one instance, he asked MBA students to choose a bespoke suit. In another experiment, he studied the behavior of real customers purchasing accessories for their new cars. As expected, initially people would carefully weigh up the choices and study a multitude of features. As they got tired, ego depletion set in, automated decision making took over, and people settled for the default option. An even more interesting finding was that by manipulating the order in which various accessories were presented, customers purchased accessories on average $1.5K more than a control group did. (Baumeister & Tierney, 2012)

So, when choosing your interviewing slot, choosing an earlier or later slot makes a big difference to your chances of being employed. As Baumeister concludes, "decision fatigue leaves us vulnerable to marketers who know how to time their sales." (Baumeister & Tierney, 2012, p. 103). Maybe we should take some time to reflect on this effect, if only for one minute during our recruitment routine. We start our morning full of energy and willpower. We interview more people, pay attention, ask questions and genuinely put the effort in. Our willpower is already being depleted. As we go through the day, the mental tiredness settles in, we have less and less willpower and we "automate" our behavior toward the evening when we have little or no willpower left. The "brain dead" feeling kicks in. What now? We pay less attention to other candidates, focus more on specific characteristics and first impressions, ask fewer questions and infer more. **In a nutshell**, we delegate more of our decision making to intuition. In effect, we allocate less chances of success to candidates as our willpower gets depleted throughout the day. Yes, as a candidate, your position within the interviewing "queue" matters.

But how far can it go?

One of the most celebrated experiments on willpower was carried out on eight parole judges in Israel. The judges were reviewing parole requests throughout the day, a very-high-stakes situation that required high integrity, lack of bias, and clear heads. The study found that 65 percent of the requests were granted after the judges have had a meal and decreased during the two hours prior to the next meal. Researchers concluded that as judges were getting tired and hungry, they reverted back to their default position of denying requests. These findings are disturbing, as they imply that the release or otherwise of convicts was determined largely not by potential good deeds performed over the years, but rather by their appointment times and the state of the judges' bellies. Judges were not at fault, either. Their intentions were good, and the intense mental effort allocated to the reviews reflected integrity. They just haven't considered that depletion in glucose levels and intense mental effort depleted willpower. In brief, this study suggests that recruiters judge the same person differently depending on, well… how hungry they are.

Findings

Fifty percent of the managers believed this factor had no influence on their decisions. This is contradicted by the studies described above.

4.2.4 Empathy

Hood (121:2009) describes the empathy/mind–reading skills as considering "what their beliefs might be and guess at which emotions they are experiencing". Hood concludes that biases occur because "we think they are like us! They too must experience the same anxieties and frustrations". However, Hood (112:2009) explains that we often misjudge feelings of other people. Specifically, people have different personalities, opinions, backgrounds that most often are unavailable to us. And Chabris and Simons (179-180:2010) conclude "unfortunately as we empathize with someone's experiences, we become less critical of the message".

Findings

Seventy-five percent of managers stated that empathy helped them make better decisions. These managers argued that empathy helps managers "that had or have a similar job role" to "…put the other person at ease and really open up thus enabling them to ascertain the character and see below the surface", and "…it allows one to create bonds of trust, it gives one insight into what others may be feeling or thinking, it helps one understand how or why others are reacting to situations, it sharpens one's people acumen and it informs one's decisions". These perceptions are a long way from findings on human biases occurring due to assumptions that "they are like us" and "as we empathize with someone experiences we become less critical of the message" (Chabris and Simons, 179-180:2011).

4.2.5 Experience

People experienced in their job make more confident decisions and recognize patterns based on previous experiences (Klein, 31:1998). Klein argues that experience allows people to use intuition and pattern recognition to form expectations and make better decisions. However, Trivers (23-24:2011) disagrees and points out that higher experience favors "illusory pattern recognition...individuals see meaningful patterns in random data". Kahneman (219:2011) referred to studies by Tetlock and concluded that "those with most knowledge are often less reliable...the person who acquires more knowledge develops an enhanced illusion of her skill and becomes unrealistically confident".

Findings

88.89% of managers stated that previous work experiences and practices help them make better decisions when recruiting employees. One manager explained, "It's always good to have previous experience in recruiting, as you will be more confident, and you will know what you are looking for in a candidate...you will be able to put yourself in their shoes and talk about your past experience". Again, managers seem to lack awareness of the relationship between experience, confirmation bias, and overconfidence bias.

4.2.6 Power

Trivers (20, 292:2011) explains that "the powerful are less attentive to others, see the world less from their standpoint and feel less empathy for them". Similarly, Kahneman (135:2011) refers to different experiments to sum up that "merely reminding people of a time when they had power increases their apparent trust in their own intuition".

Findings

87.50% of respondents believed that position of recruiters on the hierarchy ladder was not influencing recruitment decisions. Managers stated that the higher the position, the more experienced the manager was and better at empathizing with employees. As one manager explained, as they advance their careers "people get better at empathy as they go through life because they are just simply more experienced, and therefore can relate to others better". These perceptions and beliefs are contradicted by many previous studies in psychology.

4.2.7 Stereotypes

A vast amount of scientific literature confirms the existence of stereotypes. For example, experiments revealed people's biases against handicapped people or black Americans (Trivers, 146:2011) while teachers in one experiment formed predictions on the achievements of new students based on race, gender, ethnicity and physical attractiveness (Sharot, 48:2012). Many experiments have also found that stereotype threats create vicious cycles with people becoming anxious about confirming the stereotype, which leaves less room to concentrate, performing worse and "...individuals adopt the dominant stereotype regarding themselves or their group" (Trivers, 65:2011; Wilson, 207-209, 220-222:2011; Sharot, 49-54:2012, Steele,34-41:2011; Dweck,75:2007). Kahneman (147-149:2011) refers to several experiments to conclude "professional stereotypes are as alive as they were 40 years ago".

Findings

85.71% of managers acknowledged the influence of stereotypes in recruiting candidates.

4.2.8 Mood of Recruiter

Wiseman (221:2009) found that people's moods influence their perceptions of other people. And Kahneman (59-60,69: 2011) concludes that "...hearing a speaker when you are in a good mood...induces cognitive ease" and good moods "loosens the control of the conscious mind over performance – when in good mood people become more intuitive and more creative but also less vigilant and more prone to logical errors".

Findings

75% of managers acknowledged the influence of recruiter's mood in recruiting candidates, thus 25% seemed unaware of biases in relation to their mood.

4.2.9 First Impressions

Sutherland (18:2007) refers to a classical experiment by Ash to underline the importance of first impressions for decision-making purposes. Psychologist Solomon Ash experimented with two groups of people prompted to rate a person based on nothing more than a set of adjectives provided about the person. Both groups received the same adjectives, but for one of them, the positive adjectives were presented before the negative words, while the other group received the negative words before the positives. For example, the first group was presented with adjectives such as *intelligent, industrious, impulsive, critical, stubborn, envious,* while the second group was presented with the same adjectives in the following order: *envious, stubborn, critical, impulsive, industrious, intelligent.* The group receiving positive adjectives first rated the person described as more positive on attributes such as happiness or how sociable they were than the other group did. Hence, simply priming people with positive adjectives affected their overall perception and rating of the person. (Sutherland, 2007). Sutherland (19:2007) concludes that when people impressed at the beginning of a task, people assessing the task perceived the person as doing better than they actually did. As Sutherland (19:2007) explained "...when subjects heard the first words, they began to build a mental picture of the person. They then tried to make subsequent words fit in with this picture". Finally, Sutherland (20:2007) referred to several experiments to conclude that "...beliefs are formed by first impressions: later evidence is interpreted in the light of these beliefs".

Findings

88.89% of managers stated that first impressions were important and helped them make better recruitment decisions. For example, one manager stated that "this is a good time to see how the candidate comes across, do they arrive early or late, are they dressed appropriately, their body language and their communication skills. These will help you to define what type of person they are, e.g. are they serious, are they laid back and not bothered, etc." Managers lack awareness of their biases in relation to first impressions, as found by most studies in psychology.

4.2.10 Intuition

Intuition represents one skill we use to decide or form opinions about people (Hood, 40-41:2009). The effect is that "past experience and learning may be vague and unconscious, but they provide a "feels right" marker that enables individuals to be sure about their decisions" (Hood, 41-42:2009). However, Kahneman conducted numerous experiments to confirm, "the confidence people have in their intuitions is not a reliable guide to their validity" (Kahneman, 239-240:2011). Kahneman emphatically concludes that "a vast amount of research offers a promise: you are much more likely to find the best candidate if you use this procedure [a scientific approach] than if you do what people normally do in such situations, which is to go into the interview unprepared and to make choices by an overall intuitive judgment such as "I looked into his eyes and I liked what I saw" (Kahneman, 233: 2011).

Findings

88.89% of managers stated that previous experiences help them make better decisions on recruiting candidates. For example, managers believe that a higher amount of experience is correlated with an "ability to read people" while another manager explains that "intuition takes over, the gut feeling and perhaps the subconscious decisions as determined by previous experiences, sympathy".

4.2.11 Existing Beliefs and Expectations

Sutherland (105-107:2007) once stated that "the evaluation of evidence is highly biased by existing beliefs" and "...people avoid exposing themselves to evidence against their beliefs. On receiving evidence against their beliefs, they often refuse to believe it.... distorts people's interpretation of new evidence. People selectively remember items in line with their beliefs". Finally, Ariely (160:2008) concludes, "when we believe beforehand that something will be good it generally will be good and vice versa". Sharot (48:2012), Ariely (176:2008) and Bloom (44-49:2011) referred to several experiments to demonstrate that our expectations affect the way we perceive the experience and the person itself. For example, in one classic experiment, Harvard psychologist Robert Rosenthal and Lenore Jacobson, a principal at an elementary school, were looking to understand the impact that expectations of teachers had on performance of students. The researchers picked a group of students and provided teachers with a piece of information: those students had intellectual abilities significantly higher than the rest of the other students. This information was nothing else than a fabrication; there was no evidence that the chosen students had abilities different than other students. And yet, at the end of the year the joke became reality: the chosen students did score higher on IQ tests than the comparison group that scored similarly at the beginning of the experiment. Rosenthal and Jacobson concluded that people are influenced by the expectations placed on them. In this case, teachers spent more time with these "talented" students, provided them with more feedback in class, encouraged them to respond more, and overall supported them more than the "less talented" students. (Sharot, 47-48:2012) This effect was named the "Pygmalion effect" and has since been demonstrated in numerous experiments across a large variety of industry and settings. You may have observed this effect at play in a recruitment setting: for various reason, i.e., great CV, good feedback about the candidate prior to the interview, length of experience or brands worked for, age, education – these all create expectations about the candidate, the recruiter forms an unconscious decision about the candidate and needs only to confirm it (confirmation bias). As Chabris and Simmons (38, 48:2011) concluded following their Nobel winning experiments, "our experience and expectations help us to make sense of what we see and…people see what they expect to see and remember what they expect to remember"

Findings

88.89% of managers believed that prior feedback on candidates from colleagues, peers, etc., will help them make better decisions. One manager stated that "this is important as by interviewing a candidate who has been recommended, the interviewer will be interviewing a candidate that has been "shortlisted" …" Another manager explained that "… this will give you the bigger picture of how other people think the candidate works, this way you can see if they have any of the attributes you require". Hence there is lack of awareness of the impact of beliefs or expectations formed before interviewing candidates. Managers describe their bias in action and how it impacts their decisions without being aware of these biases on their own perceptions of candidates.

4.2.12 Confirmation Bias

Hood (243:2009), Trivers (153:2011), Sutherland (4,7:2007) or Suroviecki (177:2005) explained that "confirmation bias causes decisions makers to unconsciously seek the bits of information that confirm their underlying intuitions" and "once you have formed a judgment of someone you are likely only to notice aspects of his behavior that confirm it" (Sutherland, 141:2007). For example, many studies found that people intuitively lean toward asking questions that are most likely to elicit the answers they want to hear" (Gilbert, 168:2007). Remember the experiment conducted by Ash and described by Sutherland (18:2007)? In Solomon Ash's experiments, two groups of people were prompted to rate a person based on nothing more than a set of adjectives provided about the person. Both groups received the same adjectives, but for one of them the positive adjectives were presented before the negative words, while the other group received the negative words before the positives. For example, the first group was presented with adjectives such as *intelligent, industrious, impulsive, critical, stubborn, envious*, while the second group was presented with the same adjectives in the following order: *envious, stubborn, critical, impulsive, industrious, intelligent*. The group that received the positive adjectives first rated the person described as more positive on attributes such as happiness or how sociable they were than the other group did. Hence, simply priming people with positive adjectives affected their overall perception and rating of the person. (Sutherland, 2007) Sutherland (20:2007) concluded by emphasizing that numerous similar experiments demonstrated that "interviewers form an impression of the candidate within the first minute or so and spend the rest of the interview trying to confirm that impression".

Findings

88.89% of managers stated that first impressions about candidates helped them in making better recruiting decisions. While some managers showed awareness of this effect, most managers were unaware of the impact of first impressions on their recruitment decisions. For example, one manager explained that "this is a good time to see how the candidate comes across, i.e., timekeeping – do they arrive early or late, are they dressed appropriately, their body language. These will all help you to define what type of person they are, i.e., are they serious, are they laid back and not bothered, etc.". Another manager continued, "...this is very important as the candidate really needs to stand out from the other candidates. They need to be rememberable". Again, managers lack awareness of their confirmation bias, neglect to consider circumstances (i.e., why are candidates late, etc.) and believe that from a first impression they can "define" what type of person a candidate is. This confirmed Kahneman's (199:2011) findings on confirmation biases, that once we reached a decision based on first impressions, we "define" the candidate, and seek for confirmation of our initial impressions. As proven by findings in psychology, managers inferred traits of candidates from first impressions. Specifically, managers associated first impressions on dress code, body language, etc., with traits of seriousness as an example. Finally, the findings also confirmed the existence of Halo effects, as managers seemed to like or dislike candidates based on timekeeping, dress code or body language and placed similar labels on all their other characteristics.

4.2.13 Misreading Body Language

Trivers (10-12:2011) refers to several studies to explain that "people who are lying are expected to show nervousness, control (suppressing behavior, over control, overreacting), cognitive load...", however "surprisingly, nervousness is one of the weakest factors predicting deception". However, Trivers (10-12:2011) concludes that on the contrary "being suspected of lying can make you nervous regardless of whether you lie". As a side comment, self-confidence is yet another of the many factors wrongly associated with competence.

Findings

Some of the signs associated by managers with lying or hiding information were inconsistency in narrating similar events, lack of confidence, no eye contact (or cannot hold), vagueness, lack of enthusiasm, try to change the subject, take a long time to answer the question, rubbing hands, being unsettled, partially cover their mouth when they speak, nervous, not looking directly at you, scratch behind their ear or their nose, playing with their fingers/feet/biting nails. In fact, most of these cues are associated with nervousness. Of course, if we remember findings by Trivers (10-12:2011) "surprisingly, nervousness is one of the weakest factors predicting deception". Yes, managers wrongly associate signs of nervousness with deception.

4.2.14 The Hallo Effect

Kahneman defined The Hallo Effect (82:2011) as the tendency to like or dislike everything about a person including things you did not observe. Kahneman (84:2011) continues by pointing out that first impressions matter as "the Hallo Effect increases the weight of the first impression, sometimes to the point that subsequent information is mostly wasted" and resulting in confirmation biases. Specifically, Kahneman (199:2011) explains that people tend to match most qualities of a person to our judgment of one attribute that is particularly significant. Finally, Sutherland (20:2007) concludes, "if one person has a good or bad trait we tend to assume that all his other traits are good or bad". For example, if a ball pitcher is attractive, we will most likely perceive him better at throwing the ball than an ugly player that delivers a similar performance (Kahneman, 199:2011). And of course, if you are slightly late for your interview you are probably bad at your job as well…

4.2.15 Pleasantness

Wiseman (43-45:2009) referred to experiments by Chad Higgins and Timothy Judge to conclude that in an interview, pleasantness matters more in getting the job than qualifications and work experience…" For example, candidates "charmed their way to success in several ways. A few had spent time chatting on topics not related to the job, but that interested the candidate and interviewer, some had made a special effort to smile and maintain eye contact, other had praises for the organization…". Wiseman (45-49:2009) concludes that "likeability is more important than academic achievements and experience…in order to get your dream job, going out of your way to be pleasant is more important than qualifications and past work experience"

Findings

77.48% of managers mentioned that throughout the interview the candidate should be pleasant, and 62.50% believed that it was important that the candidate developed and sustained an interesting conversation not necessarily relevant to the interview. Again, managers seem to associate pleasantness and likability with knowledge or fit to the job. This confirms Wiseman's (43-45:2009) conclusion that in an interview pleasantness matters significantly more in getting the job than qualifications and work experience" and "likability is more important than academic achievements and experience".

4.2.16 Side-by-Side Comparisons

Gilbert (141:2007) shows that "we are too easily fooled by side-by-side comparisons" and "when an object is surrounded by dissimilar objects it naturally stands out" (Gilbert, 154:2007). One manifestation of side-by-side comparisons is the contrast principle, which plays to the tendency people have to perceive different products and assess them based on contrasts between the products. For example, if a second product differs greatly from the first, we perceive the second product as being more different than it actually is. (Cialdini, 2007) Psychologist Robert Cialdini tells the story of a real estate salesperson who was starting his routine by taking potential customers to see rundown properties at inflated prices. Only after this process did the real estate seller presented the house he actually intended to sell. This house was now perceived as a bargain when compared with the houses presented earlier. (Cialdini, 2007) But what must this do with recruitment? Quite a lot actually. For example, Sutherland (125:2007) points to the tendency of people of "exaggerating the qualities of a person who stands out from others..." and refers to the contrast effect to show that "if the selection committee interviews some exceptionally intelligent-sounding applicant, they are likely to underestimate the next one interviewed and vice versa" Sutherland (206-207: 2007). If you ever recruited people, you will recall the overconfident HR Manager who likes a similarly overconfident candidate and deems him as the benchmark for all other candidates.

Findings

Most managers seemed aware of the side-by-side effect described and stated that candidates are to be considered on a wide area of qualities, and assessed individually based on the job. Some managers acknowledged that if interviewing a good candidate, that candidate will set up the bar for the next one, suggesting the potential existence of side-by-side biases.

4.2.15 Conformity and Group Polarization

Suroviecki (38-39:2005) refers to a classical experiment by Ash (described below), since then replicated countless times to show that when in groups people conform and "change their opinion because it's easier to change their opinion than to challenge the group" while experiments by Sutherland (33:2007) found that "...subjects that were not influenced by other people's judgments became extremely nervous and hesitant, and experienced a fear of rejection by the group".

The classic experiment Suroviecki was referring to was conducted by Solomon Ash, a psychologist who asked participants to identify a line, out of several lines of different lengths, that matched a standard line. At the start, participants were told that they were participating in an exercise of visual perception. Within the group, all members were accomplices of the experimenters, besides the unaware subject. The subject was scheduled to answer the question on the correct line last, after all other group members had provided their answers. Throughout the experiment, the stooges were often pointing to the wrong line, even though the correct answer was obvious. As a rational person, you would predict that subjects contradicted the group and pointed to the correct line. After all, it was so obvious, right? As you have probably guessed, the body language of participants showed disbelief to the choice of the group, and yet 50 to 80 percent of the people went along with the group. (Ross & Nisbett, 2011) What this experiment also demonstrated was the principle of polarization, which is the tendency of a group of people to become more extreme in their beliefs.

From another perspective, Dweck refers to experiments proving the wide existence of the group think concept to conclude "...everyone in a group starts thinking alike...no one disagrees" (Dweck, 134:2007).   Group polarization occurs when people are constantly comparing themselves to everyone else. As Surowiecki (185-186:2005) explains "people who are uncertain about what they believe will look to other members of the group for help...but if the majority supports a position, then most arguments will be made in support of that decision". And Grovetter quoted by Surowiecki (257: 2005) argues that most people are somewhere in the middle. Their willingness to riot depends on what other people in the crowd are doing". Sutherland (44-46:2007) further explains, "if the members attitudes are biased in one direction, simply by interacting together their attitudes become even more biased in the same direction".

Findings

An overwhelming 87.50% of managers strongly agreed it was important that interviewing panel members consulted with each other, communicated impressions and agreed on final ratings of candidates. One manager believed that "consultation with another member will help compare own view with the other member's opinion, thus minimizing the subjectivity likeliness when taking a decision". Another manager argued "panel members are valuable because they can provide different perspectives on the qualifications of the candidates". Finally, in line with comments by several other managers one manager concluded "it's always good to get people's perspectives on things as your judgment will probably not be the same as others. What one person sees in someone you may miss this". This survey uncovers a large gap between current recruitment practices, beliefs and findings within the social psychology field. Managers unwarily reveal their conformity to group bias by emphasizing the importance of consulting with panel members and being influenced by their decisions. Managers are prone to the group polarization effect as they are consulting with panel members to minimize the subjectivity of their opinion, swaying, therefore, their decision depending on perceptions held by other members within the panel.

4.2.16 Professional Image of Candidates

Collins (36-37:2001) found that "boards of directors frequently operate under the false belief that they need to hire a larger than life, egocentric leader to make a company great" despite findings that the greatest leaders were quiet, humble, modest, reserved, shy, mild-mannered, understated, fanatically driven to produce results. Hence, Collins (38: 2001) concludes that wrong expectations of what great leaders should look and behave like influence recruitment decisions, with a lower number of leaders being employed vs. "larger than life, charismatic leaders". Again, the power of (wrong) associations at work: wearing an expensive suit in your interview - you must be competent; cheap looking suit – you succeed less, less competent, etc.

Findings

One hundred percent of the managers agreed that reputation of candidates plays an important role in forming initial impressions and expectations from the interviewee (i.e. caliber of the candidate). One manager explained that "of course, there is no smoke without fire (good or bad), people do change, however, feedback from peers, colleagues is a reference in itself" while another manager believes that reputation will "help you evaluate if they have the attributes you require". Another manager concludes "an initial impression and expectations are always good as it allows you to form a good first impression…" To sum up, managers are not aware of their biases and form impressions and expectations on candidates well before they actually met them. Indeed, without ever meeting the candidates, managers evaluated "if they have the attributes you require".

4.2.17 Name of Candidates

One experiment described by Kahneman (64:2011) is telling to the positive impact of easier to pronounce names on **the degree of attention** received. In one experiment, participants were asked to evaluate reports from two companies named Artan and Taahhut. Subjects gave more credit to the company they could think of more easily (Artan), presumably because they unconsciously avoided the cognitive effort of thinking about the more complicated name. (Kahneman, 2011) Another study found that companies with names that are more easily pronounceable (Emmi, Swissfirst or Comet) did better than companies with more difficult names (Geberit, Ypsomed) in the first week after their stock was issued (Kahneman, 2011). I experienced this first hand when as a training project, I was building my first website for a translation agency I was launching. After much deliberation, I went with "Bestranslations.co.uk". At first glance this seems sensible; however, at a closer look you will notice that the letter "t" is missing after "Best". Every time I was trying to type the name of my company into Google I had to make a conscious effort to stop and think about the name, adding further cognitive pressure on myself to where I simply typed "best translations" into Google. **In a nutshell**, these experiments and many other similar experiments indicate that easily pronounced names evoke a favorable attitude. Let us conclude with yet another awkward bias that emphasizes the impact of names on perceptions of candidates: several experiments referred to by Trivers (164:2011) found that letters in our first and last names or birth dates were found to positively impact the perceptions we form about a person. Trivers explains that "people prefer letters that are found in their own first and last names", an effect particularly strong for the first initials of our first and last name. The experiments are relatively simple: people are being asked to choose between two letters quickly and without time to think about it (therefore testing un-conscious biases). The results are overwhelmingly consistent: people choose the letters found within their name. The effect is attributed to the familiarity with own names. It seems that the more exposed we are to a product (or name in our case), the more we get to like the product (name); an idea referred to as the familiarity principle. The main reason for this positive predisposition to familiar products is that "repetition induces cognitive ease and a comforting feeling" (Kahneman, 2011, p. 66). Byron Sharp explains in his book *How Brands Grow* that "familiarity breeds liking. Usage also breeds familiarity and brand knowledge. This breeds liking" (Sharp, 2010, p. 91).

Findings

62.50% of managers stated that name of candidates name did not affect their decisions, unaware of the findings described above. Some managers did, however, acknowledge that names influence them "but it shouldn't...the name of the candidate influences the recruiter who may not even be aware of this" while another manager concluded that "it is difficult not to form preconceptions on other people before you've gotten to know them".

4.2.18 Curriculum Vitae

Daniel Oppenheimer carried out five studies where he reviewed the complexity of language used in various contexts, including job applications. He then presented that passages to samples of readers, and asked them to rate the intelligence of the person who has written the text. Oppenheimer found that text written in simpler language prompted the readers to rate the author higher on measures of intelligence. This has in effect confirmed that complex language sends out bad impressions (Wiseman, 51: 2009). And as CVs provide recruiters with the first impression about a candidate, it will negatively influence his perceptions, confirmation bias kicks in and voila...as a candidate you are already on the back foot. Of course, let us observe that in this case the recruiter made inferences before actually meeting you. Oppenheimer also found that factors such as the font used for writing the application prompted readers to rate candidates higher on measures of intelligence. Wiseman concludes that "you can increase how bright people think you are simply by improving your handwriting and simplifying your language" Wiseman (51: 2009).

Findings

87.50% of managers acknowledge the influence of CVs on their recruitment decisions and perceptions. Just by looking at a well-written CV, managers determined that candidates were dedicated to their career, work life is important to them, organized, prepared, a better viewing when selecting a candidate, no time waster, educated, has common sense, etc. Managers stated that badly written CVs meant that the candidate is not literate, not organized, does not work in a timely manner, does not check his/her duties to ensure that is done correctly, doesn't care about working, they don't take care or pride in what they have done or achieved, the job is not important to him/her, average intelligence, and probably not having organizational skills. Only one manager acknowledged that "this may not necessarily mean that the candidate is not the right person for the actual position as they may not have the necessary skills to write a CV as this is mainly an administrative task". Overall, it was found that managers label candidates before actually meeting them, or with little consideration to circumstances.

4.2.19 Similarity of Candidate vs. Recruiter

Duhig (220:2012) and Wiseman (62:2009) found that "regardless of whether the similarity is dress, speech, background, age, religion, opinions, personality...we like people who are like us and find them more persuasive than others". Experiments referred to by Trivers (164:2011) describe how far the similarity effect can actually go: letters found in our first and last names or birth dates were found to affect the decisions taken. And Wilson (54:2011) concludes that we like people like us because "interacting with people who share our core beliefs is a way to strengthen and validate our beliefs". The familiarity principle discussed in a previous section also affects our perceptions of a candidate–the more familiar we are with the person (whether background, experience, name and so forth) the more we feel at ease with the person. The effect? Well, studies by psychologists such as Gary Klein have found that we are more likely to compare various options with our choice when the option available to us is unfamiliar (Klein, 1999). We scrutinize an unfamiliar candidate more and compare him more against other candidates. When familiar with the candidate, intuition, and gut feeling takes over, decisions are being made on autopilot, we scrutinize less and "like" more.

Findings

Some managers acknowledged this factor as important when making recruitment decisions. As one manager concluded "a workplace is also a social place therefore to work with someone you can relate to is always beneficial as one may find it easier to tune in to the other person" while another manager explained that "this gives them more things to talk about and would take advantage of the background". And, 71.43% of managers believed it was important that candidates saw things from the viewpoint of the recruiter. As one manager stated, "Yes, it's always nice to have someone that agrees with your perspectives, as it will be easy to train, guide and manage them". However, most managers felt this factor was not crucial. Conversely, only 14.29% of managers did not consider similarity important when recruiting employees, which confirms the existence of this bias.

4.2.20 Attractiveness of Candidates

Bloom (65:2010) refers to various experiments to point that "people are attracted to good-looking faces!" while Trivers (16:2011) concluded, "...facial expressions lead to people inferring not only the emotions of the other person but also "a premonition of what she was going to do next". Kahneman (91:2011) also refers to extensive studies by Todorov to show that a simple glance at the face of a stranger results in people evaluating how dominant or trustworthy the person is. However, Kahneman (90:2011) argues that "the accuracy of mind reading is far from perfect: round chimes are not a reliable indicator of meekness and smiles can to some extent be faked". Despite this, Todorov quoted by Kahneman (91:2011) found that people associate competence with the two dimensions of strength and trustworthiness: "the faces that exude competence combine a strong chin with a slight confident-appearing smile". Bloom (13:2010) concludes that when we know how someone looks like (i.e., color of skin) we generally infer invisible facts about him (i.e. income, religion, etc.). But how about attractiveness? How does it make us feel? Let us consider one experiment carried out by psychologist James Roney who first presented groups of young boys with two pictures, one of an attractive young woman and one of an older woman. When asked to fill in surveys which measured their different attitudes, Roney found that the group presented with the image of an attractive woman valued ambition, material wealth, and status more than the control group did. (Laham, 2012) And, when in a lustful mood, men are more likely to cooperate if we go by the finding of an experiment where male skateboarders were asked to perform 10 tricks in a University of Queensland study. When the researcher was an attractive woman, the participants took more chances in performing more-difficult skateboarding tricks than they did when the researcher was a man (Laham, 2012). When the attractive researcher conducted the study, men felt more adventurous and courageous and adapted their behavior in line with their feelings. Hence, attractive people make us feel different and act different, whether we like to admit it or not.

Findings

87.50% of managers showed awareness of the influence of this factor in recruitment decisions. One manager explained that "consciously or subconsciously we are all influenced every day…" while another concluded that "appearance influences one's subconscious and so it is important that we recognize when instinct is really just prejudice". Several managers mentioned that the influence of this factor depended on the job role. For example, some managers mentioned that "the recruiter may want someone who is attractive, e.g. bar staff, air hostess, etc."

4.2.21 Spontaneous Transference Trait

Various experiments by Wiseman found that when people criticized another person, participants consistently attributed the negative traits to the speaker.

For example, in one experiment conducted by psychologist John Skowronski and his colleagues, participants were asked to watch various video clips of actors (albeit, unknown to the participants who believed the scenario) talking about third parties (presumably friends or acquaintances of the actor). When the actor would make negative comments about the third party (i.e. "He hates animals...he saw this puppy. So, he kicked it out of his way") participants consistently attributed the negative traits to the speaker (Wiseman, 57-58:2009). Conversely, if the interviewee mentions positive and pleasant things about colleagues, bosses, friends, etc., they are perceived as a more likable person.

Findings

Managers have overwhelmingly shown this bias. One hundred percent of managers believed that people who mentioned positive things about former employers, managers or colleagues have good work ethics, a potential positive addition to the present team, loyal, one who can keep integrity, a positive person. One manager associated positive comments of employees about former employers with the fact that "this states that previously he was appreciated within the company and did have a team who like him and treated him with respect leading to good feedback about the candidate about his previous employer". This is obviously a good example of the spontaneous transference trait, as only references and feedback from previous employers after the interview, rather than "talking the talk" will determine actual perception held by previous employees about the candidate. Employees that criticized former employers were labeled as a potential problem candidate, unprofessional, someone who doesn't respect the management level and their procedures, negative, inflexibility, lack of commitment to the company, he will quit this job too when something is not to his/her liking. Only one manager considered circumstances and mentioned that the candidate "may have different ideas on how things are done. This can be a good thing as they are bringing something new to the team".

4.2.22 Overconfidence of Candidate

Trivers (14:2011) explains, "overconfidence often appears to be poorly associated with knowledge – the more ignorant the individual the more confident she or he may be". In similar fashion Kahneman (45:2011) concludes his studies by stressing "many people are overconfident and prone to place too much faith in their intuitions". Furthermore, Kahneman (220: 2011) refers to his studies with psychologist Gary Klein to conclude that "...high subjective confidence is not to be trusted as an indicator of accuracy and low confidence could be more informative". Finally, Chabris and Simmons (98:2011) refer to several experiments to show that "...people take your confidence as an indicator of ability even though you are no better than your peers". Consider for example one experiment that was described by Chabris & Simons. Groups of four people who had never met before were asked to solve several math problems. Participants were first asked to take a personality test measuring how dominant they were. Researchers recorded and closely analyzed the solving sessions. They found that people with a more dominant personality had most often taken leadership of the group, even though they proved to be no more expert or competent than other group members.

So, how did they become leaders or influencers? In the words of Chabris & Simons, "The answer is almost absurdly simple...They [the dominant influencers] spoke first...people with dominant personalities just tend to speak first and most forcefully...If you offer your opinion early and often, people will take your confidence as an indicator of ability, even though you are actually no better than your peers". (Chabris & Simons, 2010, p.98) On reflection, you often experience this contradiction throughout life: incompetent bosses who talk their way into a job, group brainstorming sessions hijacked by mediocre "leaders," confident influencers and professionals who are forever "everywhere" online with nothing much to say. Yes, overconfidence pays off.

Findings

88.89% of managers identified confidence as a primary characteristic they are looking for when interviewing candidates. This indicates another gap between management practices and findings that "overconfidence often appears to be poorly associated with knowledge" (Trivers, 14:2011).

4.2.23 Inference of Traits

Sutherland (148:2007) refers to the classical "Linda" experiment, to prove beyond doubts that people have "the tendency to believe that because part of a description is true, the whole description must be true". This famous, award-winning experiment was staged by Daniel Kahneman and Amos Tverski, and provides a brilliant example of wrong associations at work. The two researchers described a person they called Linda and asked the participants whether Linda was more likely to be a bank teller or a feminist bank teller. Based on the information provided, the logic was pointing out that Linda was more likely to be a bank teller, and yet 85 to 90 percent of the subjects thought that her concerns about discrimination and feminism made her more likely to be a feminist bank teller. (Kahneman, 2011) Thus Kahneman and Tverski (157:2011) found that the unrelated factors such as the profession of a person generally leads people to (irrationally) infer behavior and personality characteristics.

CHAPTER 5.
FURTHER DISCUSSION

5.0 Is Corporate Identity Considered When Recruiting Employees?

The Management population acknowledged the role of employees to successful organizations. For example, managers explained that employees "make the difference between success and failure" or "...people within the organization are what makes an organization successful or not". Recruiting the right employees was often mentioned as well. For example, one manager stated, "employee selection is perhaps the most important part of any modern organization...the actual selection process is vital to involve the right characters for each role". Another manager also agreed, "recruiting staff is an essential part of any business...when organizations choose the right people for the job...these people not only produce good results but also tend to stay with the organization longer". Finally, another manager concludes, "an organization may have all the latest technology and the best physical resources, but if it does not have the right people it will struggle to achieve the results it requires". However, when recruiting employees considerations of operational benefits was found to take priority against the corporate identity and brand values. Specifically, most managers are too focused on matching the right skills to the right operational job, as opposed to matching the person to the organization and its identity. For example, managers stated that "...the actual recruitment process is vital to involve the right characters for the right role", "can help to match up the right person with the right job skills", "...choose the right people for the job..." These findings are in line with previous studies (Hallier and Leopold, 1996, De Chernatony and Cottam , 2008; Collins, 2001) and argue for the idea of matching the employee values to organizational values to ensure flexibility, rather than a match to the job itself. This is mainly due to potential inflexibility on the employee's part in a fast-changing world.

To sum up:

Managers acknowledge the importance of people to the success of organizations. And yet, operational needs rather than corporate identity are taken into consideration when recruiting brand people. Specifically, when recruiting, managers are looking to match a person to skills rather than a person to the organization. Of course, this often leads to bad decisions in recruiting the wrong people for the organization (but with the right skills for the job). Needless to point out that corporate identity is compromised from the start...while a person may have the skills required for the job at a particular time, as de Chernatony and Cottam (2008) stressed employees should be flexible to changes in a continuously fast-changing world. Or, as Collins (42:2001) found "great leaders understood three simple truths: you need to begin with Who rather than What...it is much easier to change direction and adapt".

5.1 Management Knowledge vs. Findings in Psychology

The survey revealed a very large gap between management knowledge, perceptions and recruitment practices vs. findings within the social psychology field. This confirms Pink's (2009) assertion about the significant "mismatch between what science knows and what business does. The gap is wide. Its existence is alarming." Specifically, when making recruitment decisions, managers assign too much weight to previous experiences, "gut feelings", empathy levels or opinions of other panel members, are overconfident in their abilities of making better decisions, and mainly unaware of biases affecting the recruitment decisions they make. They prefer candidates with similar backgrounds and views, and are unaware of biases related to their age, gender, the impact of willpower, or the impact of their own position of power. Managers are prone to inference traits biases and poorly associate a candidate's likability, pleasantness, confidence or ability to "talk the talk" about former employers with knowledge, experience, suitability for the role, achievements up to inferring character traits or performance levels in previous roles. Managers place high value on first impressions while lacking awareness of its impact (i.e., CV, name, feedback from previous employers) on forming initial expectations and beliefs about candidates, and the subsequent confirmation biases. They poorly associate signs of nervousness with deception, which makes them prone to reaching wrong conclusions about candidates. Most managers acknowledge both the effect held on their decisions by the attractiveness of candidates, stereotypes or the mood of the recruiter, "...but it shouldn't".

5.2 Overview of Findings

5.2.1 Extent to Which Objectives Were Achieved

a. *To understand the extent to which corporate image is considered and acknowledged by leadership when recruiting Brand employees.*

Managers consider mainly operational aspects when recruiting employees and generally neglect the consideration of brand values vs. employee values. The exploratory approach achieved its purpose and should provide food for thought to managers, leaders, and organizations. The idea is now available; a more thorough study within the academia is required, on a larger sample of participants in different industries. Correlated with a qualitative interview approach, this will assess perceptions held by managers and leaders at a greater extent than this current research.

b.   Evaluate the contribution of employees to the corporate image.

All previous studies stressed the impact of hospitality employees as brand "ambassadors" in aligning corporate identity to actual experiences (corporate image). Participants acknowledged the role of hotel employees to the success of organizations.

c.   Examine the effectiveness of recruitment practices in relation to corporate image.

The study found a large gap between factors considered by management when recruiting employees vs. findings on human biases. The findings confirm that current recruitment processes are inefficient. The idea is now available; a more thorough study in an academic environment is recommended, on a larger sample of participants in different industries. A scientific approach (i.e experiments) will extend our understanding in relation to the impact of human biases on recruitment decisions.

d.   Provide recommendations for improvement of recruitment practices

The first finding was that managers considered mainly operational factors when recruiting employees. Thus, the brand must increase awareness within its management community with regards to recruiting "brand people" vs. focusing exclusively on matching skills to jobs. Incorporating HR within marketing programs, redesigning recruitment practices and involving marketers in this process is, therefore, a must. This is particularly important in hospitality, given the high customer-employee interactions that affect customer's perceptions of the brand.

The second finding is that recruitment practices are inefficient; managers lack awareness of human biases in recruitment and place too much weight on factors proven to be wrong. The result stresses the importance of raising awareness within the management community with regards to these factors, their impact on recruitment, and on decision making in general. Social psychology must be incorporated within the recruitment process.

This can only start at the top of organizations by acknowledging the need for improvement, involving qualified/academic science staff in designing, incorporating and embedding new recruitment processes.

The third important finding is that contrary to popular beliefs and previous studies, management represents an effect of inefficient recruitment practices, rather than a cause of corporate identity misalignment. This includes both junior employees and managers, and as such organizations must acknowledge and treat the cause (recruitment) of failing internal marketing programs rather than the effect (employees, including managers). Indeed, the right people may not be recruited due to wrong factors being employed in recruitment (i.e. recruiters may be influenced by first impressions, similarity to candidates, believe they can empathize with candidates, other members of the panel group, etc.). Conversely, the wrong brand people may be recruited based on the biases and findings described throughout the study. And when this happens employees are disengaged, internal marketing programs fail- all leading to an inconsistent corporate image, with corporate identity messages contradicted by customers' actual experiences.

To improve congruence between corporate identity and corporate image, organizations must employ the "First Who, Then What" principle described by many studies i.e. Collins (2001). Similarly, organizations must acknowledge that having the right people on board doesn't automatically ensure its success. As Collins (74:2001) stressed, once the right people are on the bus, organizations have to "walk the talk" and "manage in such a way not to demotivate people".

5.3 Conclusion

As a general conclusion, the study places organizational identity at the heart of corporate identity, the "make or break" link that determines the success or failure of corporate identities. From this perspective, most factors found to have a significant impact on corporate identity are in one way or another linked or conditioned by employees' perception of the organizational identity. The study also challenges the idea that leadership alone is responsible for the corporate identity-organizational identity gaps and proposes leadership as an effect rather than a cause of these gaps. It is argued that recruitment practices are an integral part of a successful corporate identity. "Employing the right people" will contribute far more to a strong corporate image than corporate-led messages that do not match the actual experiences of all stakeholders. However, managers aren't considering corporate identity when recruiting new employees, and lack awareness of the human biases affecting their decisions of recruiting these employees. These practices result to employing the wrong people for businesses at all levels including leadership. As a side note, by the wrong people, I refer to people that would fit in well to an organization culture, i.e., a great leader will not fit in well in an organization that will not support his values, hence he will be the wrong employee and would not fit in.

5.4 Implications

The study re-emphasized the importance of regularly assessing employee perceptions of corporate identity, and tackling the causes of these perceptions. The study found various subcultures, identities, levels of corporate-organizational identity alignment and levels of commitment within national or international divisions, departments, sub-departments, etc. Given these findings, organizations are naive to believe in the achievement of unitary corporate identities. Instead, organizations must acknowledge that realistically, focusing on achieving complete alignment between corporate and organizational identity will affect profit negatively (i.e., more staff, give up to the flexibility offered by agency workers, investment in property, etc.), while a focus on profit will often result in "brand destroying strategies". Employees are not naive and acknowledge the importance of profit to organizations. However, organizations must to acknowledge that the higher the imbalance between its conflicting goals, such as profit and corporate identity, the higher the impact either on how employees perceived corporate identity (i.e., "we are trying to be something we are not…"; "they care only about money", the corporate identity is "fake"). As one employee noticed, values of brands and organizations, their goals and strategies "should be the same…it will help the hotel to provide better service and make more money", therefore both brands and organizations will reach their goals.

Congruency between the corporate identity within brands and organizations alone will not equate to success unless organizations will "go with what they say" – unless employees experienced the corporate-organizational identity fit, they will not commit to a corporate identity, regardless of the reputation or image of the brand.

The study highlighted many factors that contribute to the formation of subcultures within organizations. Understanding these factors represents an important tool in uncovering the sub-cultures and values within organizations, and will finally support managers in making decisions on reducing corporate-organizational identity gaps within these sub-cultures. Finally, leadership is interpreted by employees in relation to corporate identity. Unless employees perceive a fit between the values of leadership teams and the values promoted by the organization, employees will dismiss the corporate identity.

5.5 Further Implications: Recruitment

The study on recruitment stressed the importance of organizations paying attention to recruitment as the root cause for lack of employees' buy-in into the corporate identity. The study concludes that human resources (recruitment in particular) IS marketing. Specifically, corporate-driven messages represent nothing more than noise unless correct HR practices are integrated fully into the whole "marketing" effort.

Managers acknowledge the critical importance of employees to the success of organizations; however, they consider recruiting candidates an operational rather than marketing task, matching skills and people to jobs rather than to organizations. Thus, the recruitment process is inefficient from the start- the wrong people for the brand but with the right skills for the job are being brought on board. As Collins (51:2001) found, when deciding on what the "right employees" were, that great companies "placed emphasis on character attributes than on specific educational background, practical skills, specialized knowledge or work experience". Collins (42:2001) concluded, "if you have the wrong people, it doesn't matter whether you discover the right direction, you still won't have a great company. Great vision without great people is irrelevant". We have seen that most internal marketing programs fail even when significant investments are being made in making them a success. The reasons for these inconsistencies may not necessarily relate to brands not living up to its values, but rather that the wrong people are being recruited. "Wrong people" has a negative connotation, this is not the case. Specifically, an employee who talked their way throughout their career will not do well in a company focused on achievements but may do well in a highly political organization. The quiet, achievement-focused leaders that Collins was referring to will often thrive in a meritocracy lead company but fail in a highly political environment.

5.6 Findings vs. Expectations

The study reached its desired outcomes. On one side, some factors mentioned within the management literature were further confirmed by my findings. On the other side, the research produced very interesting findings vs. previous studies and provided "food for thought" for future research. The study confirmed my initial expectations (based on previous management literature) regarding the existence of an "amalgamation" of sub-cultures within organizations rather than a unitary identity. However, it was surprising to find that similarity in terms of age and length of service per se did not seem to influence employee perceptions of the corporate identity. I was expecting to find a far bigger congruency between the perceptions held by employees within individual departments. The finding of a large number of "sub-cultures within sub-cultures" has further increased my belief that achieving a unitary corporate identity is "virtually impossible". Based on previous studies and my personal experiences, I was expecting to find that corporate image, organizational image and corporate reputation affected employee perceptions and commitment to the brand. However, it was found that image or reputation would most likely affect perceptions and commitment of employees when linked to their perceptions of the organizational identity. I was also expecting that bi-polar identities would influence at least an employee's perceptions of the corporate identity if not their commitment to the brand. Surprisingly the study found that bi-polar identities seemed to hold only a minimal impact on an employee's perceptions. The findings regarding the impact of strategy, corporate structure, national cultures, the role of length of service in the formation of strong cultures, shared values and management behavior confirmed my expectations based on previous studies and personal experience. So, did the central role of recruitment practices in recruiting the right people for the brand, and its implicit impact on corporate identity.

5.7 Recommendations for Brand and Company

Employees stated that Brand values were adhered to inconsistently at Large and Small Hotel. Several factors were found to feed these perceptions.

First, employees identified large gaps between values of Brand and Company, and conflicting goals. Therefore, while Brand was mainly focused on strengthening brand identity, image and reputation, Company was perceived as being mainly focused on profit "despite causing a problem elsewhere". This situation led to conflicting strategies, with Brand trying to improve quality, consistency, etc., while Company was focused on increasing profit and adopted strategies such as cost-cutting and employing agency workers that undermined brand identity. These strategies proved to be "brand destroying" as employees dismissed and branded the identity communicated by Brand as "fake". Therefore, the first step that Brand and Company must take is increasing congruency between its values, goals and strategies. Brand and Company need to re-assess own targets, adjust expectations to a challenging but realistic level to achieve an optimum balance between their goals, balance perceived by employees as realistic and achievable. Once an agreement is reached, both Brand and Company must ensure that they "will go with what they say" as only then employees will perceive brand identity as "real" rather than "fake". Closing these identity gaps will indicate that both Brand and Company are committed to the communicated corporate identity. Re-assessing its expectations will not affect Brand, whose corporate identity is already being adhered to inconsistently. In the short-term, Company will give up what would be an acceptable level of profits. However, in the long-term, Brand will achieve an increased level of employee commitment and consistency in promoting its values, increased congruency between corporate identity- organizational identity- organizational image- corporate image, increased customer loyalty, improved reputation and, finally, increased profit from an increased number of franchising agreements. Company will not be at a loss either. While giving up a part of the profits for the short-term, Company will also benefit from increased brand reputation, image, customer and employee loyalty. On one side, Company can recruit talented, high performing employees attracted by the image and reputation of Brand. On the other side, attracting new customers is far more difficult and expensive than maintaining loyal customers. Company will benefit from the positive image and reputation of Brand in terms both of customer loyalty and attracting new customers.

Brand and Company must improve on assessing and following up on employees' perceptions of corporate identity. Brand and Company both must reveal and understand the different subcultures within the organization, their values and reasons behind different perceptions, and levels of commitment to the corporate identity. Only then, can Brand and Company take actions targeted at increasing congruency between identities of Brand vs. Subcultures. Employee surveys represent a good start in revealing subcultures at divisional and departmental levels. However, this research found different subcultures not only at a divisional, unit, and departmental level but also within individual departments and even "subcultures within subcultures". Therefore, employee surveys must be supported by a more in-depth process of investigation and analysis of these sub-cultures and followed by actions to align these sub-cultures to the desired corporate identity. From this perspective, the study revealed many factors affecting employee perceptions and commitment to Brand and represents an essential first step in enhancing management's understanding of various subcultures within Brand. Many employees stated inconsistency in leadership behavior as a primary area for improvement, and the employee survey revealed large gaps between the levels of management's commitment to live by the brand values and the personal example provided to employees from this perspective. Brands must act to increase congruency between management behavior and the communicated corporate identity.

Overall, Brand must also focus on developing its relationship with hotel owners, with a view to increasing congruency between their values, goals, strategies, and identities projected to employees. Failing to do so will further increase inconsistencies across the brand, dilute the brand and affect its image and corporate reputation. Company must acknowledge that its short-term goals and strategies affect its long-term financial health, as an inconsistent Brand reflects in loss of employee and customer loyalty, affect its image and reputation and therefore its capacity to attract high-performing employees and new customers; this generally reflects in lower profits in the long run.

However, placing the "fault" on leadership must be taken with a pinch of salt. The research on recruitment practices found very large gaps of knowledge with regards to own biases within the management population, which often leads to employing the wrong people for the business. Bad leadership is an effect of bad recruitment practices and human biases. An initial thought is that employees with recruitment responsibilities must be better trained to understanding their biases, and recruitment practices adapted to reduce the impact of those biases. This will produce better results than no training at all. However, most of the time our mental processes are operating outside of our consciousness, well beyond our awareness and deep in the subconscious. The mistaken belief that we can access our conscious mind, understand how it works, and decide freely has been named an "introspection illusion" by psychologist Tali Sharot (Sharot, 2012). Within the psychology field there is almost unanimous agreement that the subconscious is in the driving seat of our behavior. **In a nutshell, the idea** that we can access the processes that underlie our decisions, and **the idea of** conscious decision-making are mainly illusions. After a life of research in the field Daniel Kahneman explains that automatic decision making cannot be turned off at will, and biases are difficult if not impossible to prevent. Kahneman concludes that "...disbelief is not an option...you have no choice but to accept that the major conclusions of these studies are true...Priming phenomena arise in system 1, and you have no conscious access to them" (Kahneman, 2011, p. 57). Psychologist Claude M Steele also points out that: "One of the first things one learns as a social psychologist is that everyone is capable of bias. We simply are not and cannot be…completely objective" (Steele, 2011, p. 13). Furthermore, Benjamin Franklin, quoted by Chabris & Simons, states in a very emphatic manner that "There are three things extremely hard: steel, a diamond, and to know one's self" (Chabris & Simons, p. Intro).

PART 3.
ALGORITHMS VS. HUMAN RECRUITERS

1.0 Introduction

In my book Hacking Digital Growth 2025 – Exploiting Human Biases, Tools of the Trade & The Future of Digital Marketing I discussed at great length the idea that "attributing free will to humans is not an ethical judgment" (Harari, 2015, p. 283) and that advancement within the machine learning field will ultimately result in algorithms removing making digital marketers redundant. In this book, I will take the idea further by arguing that allowing algorithms to take over recruitment decisions from the highly-biased and overconfident manager or HR professional will significantly improve the fit between corporate and organizational identity, which will translate to a powerful, more unitary corporate image and reputation. One of the many examples I provided in my book on Growth Hacking was a machine learning algorithm developed by Facebook. Specifically, a study conducted by Facebook on 86,220 volunteers found that Facebook algorithms only needed 10 likes performed by a user to judge their personality better than their work colleagues could. Yes, that was 10 likes! In the words of marketer Seth Godin: "A vote is a statement about the voter not about the candidate" (Godin, 2012, p 42). And, it doesn't stop there. It took only 70 likes for Facebook to know volunteers better than their friends did, 150 likes to know them better than family members did, and 300 likes to predict their opinions and desires better than their spouses could. The conclusion of the research was that humans would be better if they ceded important life decisions to algorithms (Harari, 2015). Harari proposes that we should replace the old "Listen to your feelings" dogma with a new one: "Listen to the algorithms! They know how you feel" (Harari, 2015, p 392).

In this context and given the findings of my study on recruitment, I propose that recruitment must and will become a function performed by HR-trained algorithms that must replace the highly-biased and unprepared manager, or human resources professional.

1.1 Why Now?

If algorithms are so powerful, then why are they not widely adopted in recruitment yet, you may ask? Why do we still have to put up with the inefficiency of the current recruitment processes? Why do companies allow these practices to mess up the highly valuable asset that is corporate identity? To fully make you comprehend the reasons behind the slow adoption of algorithms vs. human recruiters, I will draw a parallel with the evolution of search engine optimization, a field that is literally the basis of machine learning. By understanding the evolution within this field, we will be in a better position to understand the slow adoption of algorithms over the function of recruitment. Do not worry if you do not fully understand some of the SEO-related terminology, as long as you understand the process of evolution within the field.

But first, let us explore a bit how many companies already use a combination of outsourcing platforms and machine AI to improve all sorts of parts within their HR workflow.

I have been arguing that talent represents the most important asset in organizations. However, finding the right talent and keeping it is an ongoing challenge, the competition for these people is high. The plethora of human biases recruiters are prone to doesn't help much either, and interferes with the goal of bringing the right people on board. Even the task of screening resumes efficiently and time-effectively remains a big challenge in talent acquisition: 52% of talent acquisition leaders say the hardest part of recruitment is identifying the right candidates from a large applicant pool. In yet another survey of talent acquisition leaders, about 56% say their hiring volume will increase that year, but 66% of recruiting teams will either stay the same size or contract. (ideal.com, 2018)

In this context, CEO of **Textio** Kieran Snyder elaborated about how AI is helping recruiters eradicate bias from the hiring process (Shanmugam , 2017). AI for recruiting is an emerging category of HR technology designed to reduce or even remove time-consuming activities like manually screening resumes.

Using artificial intelligence in HR work may not be a completely commonplace practice — but it's not exactly unheard of, either. For example, according to a survey carried out by CareerBuilder in 2017 one in 10 HR managers, in fact, state that AI is regularly being used in HR functions (CareerBuilder, 2107). More than half expect it to become a standard part of HR departments' tasks in the next five years. About (49%) of recruiters feel positive about the benefits of AI and automation on their jobs, while a small proportion of recruiters about 7% believed AI will have a negative effect.

These findigs are confirmed by a study carried out recently through the Harvard Business Review (Ramaswamy, 2017), which discovered that about 44 percent of businesses are already incorporating AI within the recruitment functions of their HR. On the same note, another recent survey by Jobvite on AI and automation (Rosten, 2017) discovered that recruiters have started incorporating AI and are expecting the best in all possible ways such as improving their jobs and talent acquisition. Indeed, companies and brands such as Grab, Chariot, Shop direct, Dennis, Zalando, Lazada Group, Thumbtack and a host of others are using AI-powered recruiting software and have witnessed a reduction in their cost per screen by 75%, also the revenue accumulated per employee has improved by 4%.

Although the ways companies utilize the technology will undoubtedly vary, recruiting, in particular, seems primed for increased AI use. Research conducted by Alexander Mann Solutions (Padua, 2017) found the majority of HR professionals — 96 percent — believe artificial intelligence could potentially enhance talent acquisition and retention.

At some organizations, it already has as we have already seen. Companies currently use AI technology to achieve a number of positive personnel outcomes, which we will briefly discuss next.

Reducing the amount of bad hires

One tech company, has created an analytics model that assesses portions of the interview process to identify candidates who are likely to become toxic employees — ones who lie, for instance — which has helped dramatically reduce the amount the company employs. With nearly three in four organizations reporting they've hired the wrong person for a role in the past year, at an average cost of $14,900 per bad hire, according to CareerBuilder, companies can likely make an argument for at least testing out artificial intelligence in HR functions that relate to hiring. (Josh Bersin, Laurence Collins, David Mallon, Jeff Moir, Robert Straub , 2016)

Capturing candidates who fell through the cracks

Talent rediscovery, a practice in which companies use software to screen previous applicants for open positions, may help employers find candidates in high-demand talent pools — which LinkedIn's 2016 Global Recruiting Trends (LinkedIn, 2016) report said is the biggest challenge for corporate HR departments. Given more than a third of hiring managers spend less than a minute reviewing resumes, and nearly one in five spends less than 30 seconds, according to a recent survey, chances are, some qualified candidates have been inadvertently skipped over.

Pinpointing the ideal person for a position

Instead of using AI technology to assess external hiring options, some HR departments are utilizing it to identify and recruit internal candidates for roles — such as Bridgewater Associates, a hedge fund company with an app that lets employees rate colleagues on certain attributes during meetings. In a 2017 TED Talk (Dalio, 2017), Bridgewater co-founder Ray Dalio said the Dot

Collector app helps reduce the influence opinions can have on decision making by highlighting a group consensus of how a discussion is going — and also gives the company a sense of employees' individual characteristics and how they think, which can be used to match them with the best set of responsibilities.

In another case of AI incorporation in HR, interesting job descriptions are written by recruiters through the use of a software known as Textio. This augmented writing platform compiles various job postings and puts forward to consideration suitable content to encourage the submission of more applications from job seekers.

The **Montage** software enables candidates for various job vacancies to schedule their interviews, allowing them to choose a time must suitable for them and also provides a chance to reschedule.

AI powered software such as **Stella** match suitable candidates to jobs through the tracking of experiences, credentials and qualities sought for by employers. (Beamery, 2018)

In recent years, companies' use of technology in recruitment has ranged from building a corporate alumni network to executing a social media-based employer branding strategy, sometimes involving non-traditional social media venues.

Employers have focused on mobile recruiting efforts and sponsored unique online recruitment campaigns; some have also utilized technology to share their diversity and inclusion program successes with current employees, potential candidates and the general public.

But there have been a fast leap in the use of AI by various companies to help hire and fire employees. The bot workers are scouring through employee feedback surveys to read people's feelings and pick up on their negative personality traits. Forget about robots nicking your job, they could soon be charged with hiring and firing you instead.

Truth is, an increasing amount of companies are tapping artificial intelligence to help with the recruitment process and to analyse staff sentiment. (Moise, 2018)

One of these AI systems is called Xander, which its creators claim can help employers "understand not only what their employees are saying, but how they're actually feeling". Yes, it has gone from watching you to scanning your emotions. At a steel processing company in Manhattan, Kansas, Xander is busy crunching employee feedback surveys to gauge feelings. Creepy right? But it solves the problem of identifying the mental state of employees.

The software does this by combing through blocks of text, picking up on answers to open-ended questions, and assigning attitudes or opinions to workers. After lapping up the data, Xander can determine whether an employee feels optimistic, confused or angry.

"One of my lowest scoring items was maintaining my composure under stress," said a top executive at the firm, known as SPS Companies Inc., about the feedback he received.

An AI can rapidly scan thousands of employee surveys to find out staff sentiment. On the plus side, Xander reported that the manager's staff thought he was fair and honest.

Another reason employer's are so enthralled by AI is the boost in productivity it offers. Before Xander's arrival, it took the HR team at Memphis' First Horizon National bank three months to rummage through 3,500 employee surveys. Using the AI, the bank's personnel could cut through the feedback as soon as the survey closed. Privacy concerns aside, the software has had some positive affects.

First Horizon learned that it needed to work on its training programme, and steel company SPS improved its health care plan.

Although employers have used tech to track employee actions for years, more businesses are now turning to machine learning. More than 40 percent of employers globally have implemented AI processes of some kind. (Josh Bersin, Laurence Collins, David Mallon, Jeff Moir, Robert Straub, 2016)

I will later argue the case that the current trend of outsourcing is one step away from automation. Let us look to some further cases studies of how companies used outsourcing and in some cases A/I and Machine Learning in HR and recruitment.

Intercontinental Hotel Group (IHG): Artificial Intelligence For Recruitment of Graduates

HR managers at the Intercontinental Hotel Group Europe noticed that a high number of candidates who did well during their first interview then faltered when re-interviewed by a different manager. That's when the early careers manager at IHG approached Cognisses to develop a template for the recruitment process which included a mix of classic psychometric tests and cognitive tests in the hope that the best trainee managers - and those with the higher chance of engaging in a successful career with the company - would be those who did well on the test. By using these tests, the human bias was largely wiped out. After analysis of the data provided by the Cognisess program, in 95% of the cases the right candidate was selected. This means that Artificial Intelligence was not completely able to eliminate the bias, leaving what is known as the machine bias. At the moment, it is acknowledged that no technology is capable of removing prejudice completely; in fact, a 2011 study found that machine learning could amplify the problem. This is because the algorithm is capable of picking up on gender, for example, by looking into the person's participation in certain activities. Despite the potential for machine bias, the high success rate of the recruitment process shows that artificial intelligence supersedes a more manual recruitment process as there's far less scope for error.

Roche Diagnostics, Belgium

Blockchain is a platform that was developed by IBM initially to look after various financial functions within a business. However, this machine learning software has found its way on to HR managers' desks. In this case, the program is used for traditional HR functions, such as executing contracts and managing payroll. 40% of HR managers in Europe find it difficult to provide data that will effectively support business decisions; (sdworks, 2018) therefore 15 to 30% of hiring costs goes to 3rd parties (Verlinder, 2018). Other HR functions that can be fulfilled by this type of software include the analysis of employee performance.

Roche Diagnostics Belgium used Blockchain in order to analyse absenteeism and help monitor employee mobility.

Another function in which algorithms were used in this business was to analyse the rate at which holidays were booked, thus enabling team leaders to help out employees wanting to re-establish a work-life balance.

In this case, algorithms and machine-learning are used to help measure employees' well-being.

However, Roche Diagnostics Belgium has predominantly used algorithm data as a tool that would add to a discussion around the HR function.

The software solution is better for managing employee attendance as all the absences are logged in one place, there is, therefore, less scope for human error because managers can access diaries and holiday requests all in one place. This allows them to allocate holidays in a fairer way and reduce staff turnover, because the software enables employees to regain control over their work/life balance.

Alphabet: Algorithms used for cost control and employee attendance

Alphabet was looking for an HR solution (Octopus HR, 2018) that would allow for cost-control and the monitoring of employee attendance, as no reliable records were kept prior to the roll-out of the software solution. This meant the business was unable to evaluate the cost of employee absence.

Following the implementation of the HR machine learning software, Alphabet was able to track attendance rates more accurately. The system will automatically compile attendance statistics for every employee in the business, therefore allowing for optimal attendance rates and considerably contributing to the reduction of absenteeism.

The success of tracking attendance rates using algorithms then prompted Alphabet to use the Octopus HR software solution to monitor holidays and allow employees to share their diaries more easily, thus allowing for a partial take-over of the HR function.

Not only is the system user-friendly, it also avoids any errors such as a clash in holiday dates or errors in processing the payroll. This means algorithms and artificial intelligence allow the business to run more efficiently as it helps optimise staff attendance rates. It also helps managers improve employee well-being by better distributing holiday allocation, as the use of artificial intelligence avoids any clashes.

1st Franklin Financial: A/I used to streamline the HR Process

1st Franklin Financial is a company which has a headcount of over 1,100. They hire over 250 employees each year and their previous HR function used very manual processes, such as Microsoft Excel and countless pieces of paperwork. That meant they were looking at a solution that would help streamline the process so that Human Resources could take decisions that were based on data, rather than simple judgement, while also allowing for information to circulate efficiently between employees in each of their 274 offices across six US states. The PMG system 1st Franklin Financial chose allowed them to update all employee details such as payroll, scheduling annual reviews and training certifications automatically. The system is a one-stop portal in which employees can view all the information they need regarding the business.

What's more, due to the high number of staff being hired, the company was also able to streamline its new hire process by automating part of the induction process, thus allowing new employees to settle into the business quicker and become more productive. The integration of artificial intelligence has meant fewer errors in the recruitment of new personnel as it eliminates the human bias. Furthermore, the use of AI during the induction process not only frees up the manager's time, but also allows new recruits to be productive straight away. Replacing some of the menial HR tasks with bots allows for more efficiency within the business as these are less error-prone when being made to file CVs or to schedule interviews. (PMG, 2018)

Machine Learning Used To Create An Agile HR Function (Workday, 2018)

UK internet service provider Talk Talk adopted machine learning in order to create a system that would allow all of its employees to access vital HR information.

This, combined with an outdated recruitment tracking system and the fact employees had to go through a series of manual steps to complete even the simplest of HR tasks, meant that the company chose to turn to machine learning in order to optimise its HR functions.

From a user point of view, the system offered a one-stop shop for all employees' HR needs. They are now able to consult the employee handbook, book holidays and check for training in one place, therefore totally eliminating the need for a paper trail.

This proved particularly popular; within days of the system launching, 90% of Talk-Talk employees had logged in. What's more, the system is also accessible remotely and thus empowers staff to take vital decisions regarding their career with much more ease.

Aside from being very popular among the staff, the new HR platform also enabled Talk-Talk to run its HR function more efficiently, eliminating errors in the payroll process and better managing staff as a whole.

The algorithm saved the Human Resources department a considerable amount of time, as it now spends 65 to 70% of the time developing its strategy for all areas of the business, including recruitment.

Furthermore, the adoption of the Workday algorithm by Talk Talk has also made the recruitment of new staff much easier. The system is able to view LinkedIn profiles and file CVs more accurately than a single person, therefore contributing to streamlining the recruitment process. Not only is external recruitment made a lot easier, but it has optimised the internal recruitment process too. The system has made it easier for managers to discuss the eventuality of moving an employee to a different team as the system tracks employee performance, by for example keeping a trace of employee appraisals, as well as CVs and attendance rates. The Workday platform has been successful in allowing the HR department to delegate tasks that are not necessarily their responsibility and allows team managers to make decisions based on data, thus contributing to a higher productivity and reducing staff turnover because decisions can be made based on data provided by the algorithm, which has meant getting rid of human input for tasks such as payroll management and CV filling.

Industry 4.0 used for staff retention

Staff turnover and employee retention are issues for many businesses these days, particularly with the widespread proliferation of online job boards and professional social media networking sites such as LinkedIn. That's why it's believed that bots may replace up to 24% of HR jobs by 2022 (Coleman, 2018). What's more, the recruitment process is made much easier by the use of Applicant Tracking Software. All these challenges mean that HR departments are now facing an uphill battle to simply retain valuable members of staff.

However, machine learning, AI and algorithms allow HR functions in all industries to keep track of employee progress and enable them to reward those which are worthy of being promoted, as all the information about that employee is stored in one place. That's how pharmaceutical giant Sanofi used artificial intelligence and algorithms. It enabled the HR department to move staff across different business units within the group across a variety of countries, therefore, greatly contributing to the career development of Sanofi staff. Prior to the implementation of a digital solution, it was difficult for the HR department to operate such a policy, because it was unable to analyse where the employee's talents lay efficiently, therefore exposing themselves to a too high level of risk in the decision-making process. The digitisation of the department has allowed it to have all the information relating to every employee in the business in one place. This means they can easily go and look at past appraisals, CVs and LinkedIn profiles in order to facilitate career development.

Thanks to algorithms, employees are able to have a long career within the business as digital technology allows managers to offer staff opportunities they would otherwise have to seek in another business. Therefore, staff turnover is considerably reduced and employee wellbeing is very much increased because they are able to develop their career in an environment in which they are already comfortable and in which they know they can thrive. Offering staff the chance to pursue career opportunities abroad also represents a great opportunity for personal development for employees and their families. All of this wouldn't be possible without algorithms and artificial intelligence because of the length of time it would have taken using more traditional HR processes.

Experts and employment lawyers did however warn that AI may contain biases that could lead to workplace discrimination. A hiring algorithm may notice an uptick in absences for people with disabilities and recommend against hiring them, WSJ noted.

AI has advanced in leaps and bounds in recent years, leaving regulators struggling to keep up. That may explain why the Equal Employment Opportunity Commission, the US body that enforces laws preventing workplace discrimination, hasn't announced official rules determining how AI can be used in HR decisions. However, it did suggest that the software could create new barriers for opportunities. The companies behind the tech are also grappling with its implications.

1.2 Case study: Search Engine Optimization

Those early days when Google took the Internet by storm seem far away now. From the very beginning, marketers vied for the commercial advantage of "owning" the first position in Google search results. Indeed, entrepreneurs, business owners, brand owners, and marketers all jumped at the opportunity of leveraging the power of this new and exciting publicity channel. The golden era of SEO (search engine optimization) had begun. As always, entrepreneurs and companies had plenty of help at hand from a myriad of SEO geeks that single-handedly ranked websites on the first page of Google results, making and breaking businesses almost overnight. And how would many of these great SEOs go about it? Well, the most common SEO practices included building thousands of links from unreliable sources such as link farms, press releases and directories, stuffing meta titles, meta descriptions and meta keywords, stuffing URL descriptions, and obsessively stuffing keywords into web pages. It did work for a time, mainly due to three factors. First, disciplines such as machine learning or AI were still in an emerging stage, and in spite of being around for a while AI development as a profession went through its ups and downs. An initial exuberance over its potential faded between 1960 and 1973 when it became apparent that the initial hype was not being complemented by significant advancements in the field. This led to AI researchers struggling to get funding between 1974 and 1980. However, AI was brought back on the map when Japan launched its Fifth Generation Computer System Project. The interest continued, and since 1990 funds have increasingly been invested in addressing various AI challenges. (Chace, 2015) Second, the capability of computers to store and process data increased exponentially as compared with the low processing power at that time. Third, the amount of data available in digital form was very low compared with the amount available now. In brief, Google's access to data was limited, and the processing power of computers was low. For these reasons, to determine the relevancy of a website Google unwillingly had to rely on ranking signals that were mainly under the control of webmasters. It seems unnecessary to point out that SEOs employed various questionable, albeit creative, practices, and websites often ranked high by Google were not best suited to the requirements of the user, thus impacting negatively on user experience. The advantage of a high ranking meant big money for entrepreneurs and companies who realized that in order to beat the competition they did not have to produce the best product but rather they just had to employ the best SEO services. Anyone who was exposed to SEO in its early days remembers the aura of wizardry surrounding the profession, due to the control SEOs had over the ranking factors. Indeed, the myth was born that good SEOs could wave a magic wand and magically rank your website on the first page in Google. One digital marketer known to this author recalls the story of his becoming a star overnight within his company after ranking the company website on the first page in Google. But, all he had to do was change several meta titles, meta descriptions and headings in a not-very-competitive industry. Yes, times were good for an SEO profession that was flourishing, and with it many mediocre businesses were flourishing as well. . Enter the scene Google Ads, served in the right hand column of organic search results, which were placed in the middle column. The privileged position in the center of the page ensured that the benefits of ranking organically in Google were largely unaffected by the introduction of Google ads. For example, a 2006 heat map study found that search results low down in the page received very little attention when compared with results higher up the page (Enge, Spencer,

Stricchiola & Fishkin, 2013). Furthermore, the right hand side paid ads were receiving an even lower amount of attention. This finding, of course, resulted in a loss of revenue potential for Google, which was already starting to test various elements of their ads for the purpose of maximizing revenues. Fast forward to today and the power balance has changed; SEOs have far less control over factors impacting the ranking position of websites within Google. In fact, most ranking signals considered to be essential in the past play very little or no direct role in ranking websites at present. For example, backlinks are still important, but long gone are the days when you submitted your mediocre website to hundreds of directories and link farms and got well ranked within Google. In fact, this practice would now do more harm than good to a website. Or let's consider the advice offered by SEOs for optimizing images on a page. In *The Art of SEO* the authors provide the following advice: "A descriptive caption underneath the image is helpful...Make sure the image filename or image src string contains your primary keyword...Always use the image alt attribute". (Enge, Spencer, Stricchiola & Fishkin, 2013, p. 415) And all SEO tools point to the lack of alt tags as a technical issue. Some of them like YOAST's plugin even go as far as providing information on whether the images on page include or not include your keyword within alt text descriptions. The idea behind this is that images will further improve usability and enhance a website by providing Google with information about the image and implicitly about the theme of the page. And yes, Google cannot read images but relies on webmasters to inform its algorithms about the content of images via alt text, text around the images, captions, and so forth. Thus alt tags are yet another signal that can be easily manipulated. As an example look no further than the images you purchase via services like Shutterstock where an image acquired by 1,000 webmasters is optimized in 1,000 different ways.

But what can Google do? After all, Google can't read images, right? Or can it? Actually, as early as 2012 Google's algorithms have taught themselves to recognize cats within images, without humans ever teaching the algorithms about cats! (Chace, 2015) Other examples include Google correctly classifying a picture of a boy riding a motorbike as "boy riding a motorbike on a dirty road", and an image of two pizzas on a stove as "two pizzas on a stove". And both Google and Facebook **are now able to** glance at an image and correctly identify the name of the person in the image. (Kelly,2016) **In fact,** Facebook has developed a system formed of nine levels of artificial neurons than can determine with an accuracy of 97.25% whether two images are showing the same person or not, only slightly lower than the accuracy achieved by humans at 97.53%. (Ford, 2016) Finally, as early as 2011 a deep learning neural network designed at the University of Lugano performed better than humans when it correctly identified 99% of the images from a database of traffic signs. (Ford, 2016) Looking for more hints? Improvements in face recognition technology **has given confidence to** the US Department of State to implement a facial recognition system for visa processing purposes, and many advanced surveillance systems already employ machine learning algorithms and data mining technologies to analyze large quantities of voice, video, or text. (Bostrom, 2016)

But how about more-complex digital assets like audio recordings? Well, recordings of conversations can already be analyzed by topic, voice tonality, and fluency vs. silence. (Mar, 2015) Given the improvements of speech to text technologies, recordings can also be downloaded in a text format and further sentiment analysis performed. You only need to think of the great advancements achieved by Google's Translate algorithms: simply point a device toward the speaker of another language and have that language translated to your own in real time. Sure, the system is not perfect; however, it is only a matter of time until it is. For example, Google Translate has **already** achieved almost perfect accuracy between English and Portuguese. How about video analysis? Technology is already available to recognize faces, behavior, situations, and even words within videos. (Marr 2015) **In fact,** in the past Google applied for a patent on a face recognition process, while Facebook confirmed that their face recognition algorithms now recognize faces almost as accurately as humans do (Marr, 2015).

So, what does this mean for recruitment practices?

The obvious effect of the explosion of data available in a digital format, and the increased ability of algorithms to analyze it is that algorithms will in the not too distant future develop the capability to probe your narrative and presentation during an interview against your digital profile (compiled from the vast amount of information available online). So if the company you applied for is looking for trustworthy and reliable employees, delete those Facebook images with a bull running behind you at Pamplona, when you were supposed to be at work...your WhatsApp or Gmail emails bragging about your "clever" strategy of calling in sick may just give you away, just as Facebook's algorithm recognizing your face in the crowd may **do as well**.

1.3 A Bit of History

But how did it happen, how did SEOs lose influence with Google? **More importantly**, who will win the battle for ranking your website: the creative, technical SEO professional or Google? The question of SEO vs. algorithms is of paramount importance in providing an answer to our Algorithms vs. Human Recruiters Dilemma. If Google's algorithms developed to a point where they could determine the relevancy of a website better than a human can, then it can certainly perform better in recruiting than humans. To dive more into it, this scenario signifies that Google could interpret better than humans all the complex elements within a website: text, images, videos, audio, context, feelings, and more. Similarly, Google would get better than humans at interviewing a candidate without the biases displayed by human interviewers.

To answer to these questions, let us dig a bit deeper into the three main factors that have driven the advancement of Google's machine learning algorithms: big data, computational improvements, and advancements in AI.

1.3.1 Big Data

We started this chapter by recalling the initial low bargaining power Google held over SEOs. Indeed, Google was relying on webmasters themselves to provide as much information as possible to help determine the relevancy of their websites. Besides the underdeveloped state of the machine learning arm of AI, the matter was made even worse by the fact that at the time most data had yet to be digitized. Indeed, only 25% of the whole world's data was stored in digital form. (Ross, 2017) Hence, Google's ability to learn from that relatively small set of digital data was limited, and this was in addition to unreliable ranking signals being easily manipulated by webmasters. But the new digital era had begun, an era marked by an abundance of old data appearing in digital format, massive amounts of data being produced daily, and computing power reaching levels never before thought possible. From the 25% in 2000, the proportion of data in digital format grew to 94% by 2007. (Ross, 2017) Consider a 2013 IDC Digital Universe study referred to by Marr, which stated that out of the 22% of information "ready for analysis" within the whole universe, only 5% was being analyzed, and IDC's prediction that the "ready for analysis" data proportion will increase to over 35% by 2020, while 10% of the data will be actively used for analysis. (Marr, 2015) In a nutshell, big data is going to become even bigger, and by 2020 an estimated 1.7 megabytes of data will be created every second for every inhabitant of our planet. (Marr, 2016) Google is well placed to take advantage of our willingness to share more and more data, if you consider its current web index alone is believed to be over 100 petabytes of data, comprising details of an estimated 35 trillion web pages. (Marr, 2015) Let us conclude by saying that big data is a "catchall phrase used to describe how these large amounts of data can now be used to understand, analyze, and forecast trends in real time." (Ross, 2017, p. 154)

But where is Google getting all its data from?

Let me start by pointing out that **it is not my intention to** analyze every single source used by Google to build someone's personal digital file. And even if I wanted to do that, realistically it would be impossible for anyone but Google to identify all such sources. My intention is simply to draw awareness to the increasingly large amount and the variety of data fed into Google's RankBrain algorithm. This will help us gain a better understanding of the progress Google has made over the years. **Most importantly**, this will provide us with an understanding of Google's strategic direction, and its direct impact on the task of recruiting people. Time to provide a first hint: if you take one point from this book it should be that Google is not in the business of **search at all. In fact,** Google is not in the business of social media and blogging (Google+, Blogger, Feedley, Hangouts, and so forth), email (Gmail), TV (Chromecast), Maps (Google Maps), cellphones (Pixel), books (Google Books), images (Google Images, Google Photos), news (Google News), translations (Google Translate), videos (YouTube), Contacts, Google Calendar, Google Docs, an apps store (Google Play), or any other similar applications of its technology. And Google is far from disinterested when providing developers with API access to most of their applications. We use Google's tools and applications day in day out because they **do make** our lives better. The one question we do not ask is: why is Google investing in these applications just to offer them free? The same question is pertinent for many other companies whether their name be Facebook, LinkedIn, Microsoft, or anything else. As users and marketers we got the whole thing wrong. **We think about** Gmail as a competitive response to Microsoft's Outlook, **we think** about Google+ as a response to Facebook, Chromecast as a response to Samsung's Smart TVs, and **we think** about Contacts, Gmail, and Google Calendar as productivity tools. Similarly, **we think** about Google Maps as a tool helping us navigate around town, while news feeds via News or Feedly allow us to personalize our stream. APIs are a god-sent gift, and thousands of digital marketing tools are being built both by white hat and black hat marketers leveraging Google's APIs. And, of course Google's search engine needs no introduction, if you are anything like me you cannot survive without it. For Google though, its search engine, APIs and all other applications we have been discussing are simply a means of achieving its real goal. David Kelly got this right when he pointed out that in assessing the relationship between search and AI we seem to have got it backward. Indeed, we believe that AI is being used to improve our search results when in fact Google is using its search engine to train its AI. (Kelly, 2016) Yes, we are talking about Google's RankBrain algorithm, which has already found its way into the top three ranking factors in Google. This should come as no surprise, as Larry Page, one of the founders of Google, stated as early as May 2002: "Google will fulfill its mission only when its search engine is AI-complete. You guys know what that means? That's Artificial Intelligence". (Chace, 2015, p 18)

To emphasize, Google is not in the business of Search at all. In fact, Search is simply a mean rather than an end; in our case the end is AI capability. Similarly, Google has no intention of becoming a cellphone, productivity, book, or TV company. Data and only data is at the heart of every initiative taken by companies like Google and Facebook. With this in mind, I hope I have convinced you that the vast amount of information collected via free services and applications represent the Holy Grail for Google, Facebook and the like. And, if we go by extensive statistics provided by Marr in his wonderful book *Big Data*, the ROI from these initiatives is impressive by all standards. Indeed, consider that as long ago as 2013, more than a billion tweets were being sent every 48 hours, one million accounts were being added to Twitter every day, 293,000 updates were being posted on Facebook every minute, and 172,800 new members were joining LinkedIn every day. Furthermore, the average Facebook user created 90 pieces of content, including links, news, photos, notes, and videos every day. Every minute an estimated 571 websites were being created and Tumblr owners published approximately 27,778 new blog posts, and three million new blogs were being created every month. (Marr, 2015) And, **of course,** 350 million photos were uploaded to Facebook each day, three-and-a-half million photos were uploaded to Flickr every day, 100 hours of video was uploaded to YouTube every minute, over 45 million pictures were uploaded to Instagram every day, and since June 2013 Instagram users have shared **more than 16 billion** pictures. The cherry on the cake is that 72% of adults online use social media networking websites with little or no privacy control over their activity. For example, 25% of Facebook users never bother with any **kind of** privacy control. (Marr, 2015) **Furthermore,** six of the ten most popular websites rely on user-generated content for their popularity (Brynjolfsson & McAfee, 2016).

By now, I hope you have started to reflect on the extent of your contribution to the feeding and training of algorithms such as Google's RankBrain. With all this in mind, let us now turn to some applications Google provides, and our role in training RankBrain. Again, I intend to invite self-reflection to the **amount of** information that an algorithm can hold about a candidate vs. the highly inefficient gut feeling of human recruiters, as this will help us better understand the future.

Google+, Blogger, and Hangouts

Google tracks data related to webpage visits and mainly infers personal characteristics and behavior from browsing habits. Its main competitor, Facebook, has access to a more varied palette of personal data, such as where we live, work, and play, how many friends we have, what we do in our spare time, and so forth. (Marr, 2016) **Of course,** Google also wanted a piece of the pie, hence the launch of such services as Google+, Blogger, and Hangouts.

Chromebook

Could Google compete with established players such as JVC or Samsung in the TV arena? Probably not, nor has Google had any intention to move in this direction. However, Google had somehow to get its hands on all that juicy data: what you watch, when you watch, for how long you watch, how often you stop watching, and so forth. What were Google's options? Start building TVs to compete with Samsung? Or, maybe, another business model to compete with Netflix? Either of those two options would have been a distraction from its core business, in a competitive industry where Google would struggle against Samsung, Panasonic, Netflix, NOWTV, Amazon Movies, and other major players. The solution was Chromecast, described in Next Tech magazine's "Google Tips & Tricks" as "an incredibly cheap device which can completely change the way you watch online content.... Apps like YouTube, iPlayer, or Play Movies are supported, and the process is as simple as tapping one icon". (Next Tech, 2017) Of course, many other partners include NowTv, ITV, Channel 4, and yes, even Netflix. The same magazine goes further, explaining that Chromecast is Google's answer to Apple TV, a misconception we have already discussed. Indeed, Google is competing with Apple but the prize is the rich amount of data insights rather than the TV business per se. This new move now provides Google with further data insight into your behavior: which icons you click on, what shows and movies you stream, what channels you prefer, how long you watch for, demographic information, and probably much more. To leverage the trend of cellphone overtaking desktop use, Chromecast also integrates with your Android or Apple phone or tablet. In a similar fashion, Google's Wi-Fi Home System is not competing with BT, Virgin, or other Internet providers for the delivery of Wi-Fi services. In fact, Google Wi-Fi leverages your modem and Internet provider services to amplify the Internet connection throughout your house, and once connected, more data is being collected about you, your behavior, habits, and preferences. Yep, Google tries hard to make it as easy as possible for you to feed its RankBrain algorithm.

Gmail

Gmail has become a part of daily life for many of us, and we are often grateful to Google for providing us with free access to this tool. However, did you know that, with the free version of Gmail, Google reads and analyzes all emails you are sending and receiving from your Gmail account? (Marr, 2015) You probably didn't. Hence, next time you **send an email** bragging about your clever "call in sick strategies" or about your boss, **you should** really think twice about the wording.

Waze

Waze was acquired by Google in 2013 for over a billion dollars and, at its core, it offers traffic information and recommendations to users based on information collected from other Waze users. In brief, you feed data such as your location or how fast you are moving into Waze's algorithms. Again, a great opportunity for Google to collect information on your daily behavior.

Google Pixel phone.

Mobile is big, given that of the world population of over seven billion, six billion have cell phones. (Ross, 2017) **In fact,** mobile is so big that Google **has started to move** its search index to mobile. And nowadays a website that is not mobile-friendly will find it nearly impossible to rank on the first page in Google. Is the company trying to enter the mobile business? By now, you know that Google's decision to move into the mobile market was driven by the massive volume of data generated via mobile. A similar approach was taken by Microsoft, which tried to break into the mobile business by acquiring Nokia. After failing to win a significant market share in the mobile market, Microsoft developed Windows 10 as a common platform serving desktop, tablet, and phone. (Marr, 2016) **Of course,** Windows 10 provides Microsoft with data about users, their online activities, and their behavior as users. Back to Google: we can now reflect on some of the data insights Pixel might be collecting about us. Eye-tracking data, what we click on, when we click, our browsing history, applications we download, games we play, and so on. A more robust example is that of a mobile company called Sprint, which is using data from over 55 million mobile devices to better customize ads served to users' phones. In

addition to the actual mobile phone, the company uses data about the usage of the actual device: the text messages you send, phone calls, apps usage, emails, and so forth. This option is available on an opt-in-only basis, however, Jason Delker, their chief of technology acknowledges that most other mobile companies include everyone automatically. (Marr, 2016)

Google Wallet

From the same Next Tech magazine "Google Tips & Tricks" article: "Set up Google Wallet in order to pay for purchases...It has never been easier to shop online, and Google is making strides to ensure that it gets easier by the minute". (Next Tech, 2017) Yes **indeed,** Google is making it **as easy as possible** for itself to learn about your purchasing behavior. The size of the prize? Google can now collect information on your earnings, how you spend your money, where you spend it, variations in your income, and more.

Google Books

A wealth of data is being generated about what we read, how long we read for, whether we skip pages, what pages we annotate, which ones we highlight, and any other details you can think of. (Marr, 2015)

Application programing interface (API)

Google, Amazon, eBay, and Facebook openly encourage **all sorts of communities** to interact with their platforms. Developers, marketers, and vendors are examples of people abandoning control **over the use of** their data in return for access to the capabilities developed by those companies. Consider for example that over half a million apps have been built leveraging access to Facebook's APIs. (Marr, 2016) Regardless of the purpose **any of** these integrations may have, data companies such as Google learn a great deal about the way you use their platforms.

Nest

Google acquired Nest in 2013 in what was signaled by the press as an attempt at creating an operating system for the home. One can draw a parallel with Windows 10, but for the home. Whatever the reason for the acquisition, one thing is clear: Google now has access to a wealth of information related to your temperature preferences throughout the day, when you arrive or leave home, and your overall habits. And the Google tradition of making it **as easy as possible** for you to provide data continues: Nest can easily integrate with 3rd party internet of things (IoT) devices like washing machines, smart wall plugs, fitness trackers, and smartwatches. (Marr, 2016)

Google's other stuff

Google Calendar: Google has access to data on your habits, schedule, acquaintances, and much more. **Google Maps***:* At the very minimum Google will know where you are when you are there, and how often you are in that place. **YouTube**: Google can access a wealth of data on what you watch, how often you watch, how long you watch for, and so forth. **Google Docs**. The easiest **type of** digital data to analyze is text. **Google Search**: Need I say anything?

At the time of this writing, Google's products page lists 104 items, including Google Search, Pixel phones, Daydream VR, Google+ social, Google Duo video-calling app, Google Docs suite, Google Scholar. (Google Products, 2017) **The truth is,** we could go on and on almost without end about the ways Google collects data and feeds it to its algorithms.

But what types of data are you feeding into Google's machine learning algorithms? Well, what better source for that information than Google's own Privacy policy?

Google's privacy policy

"Here are the three main types of data that we collect:

*Things **that** you do*

When you use our services—for example, carry out a search on Google, get directions on Google Maps, or watch a video on YouTube—we collect data to make these services work for you. This can include:

- Things **that** you search for

- Websites **that** you visit

- Videos **that** you watch

- Ads **that** you click on or tap

- Your location

- Device information

- IP address and cookie data

*Things **that** you create*

If you are signed in with your Google Account, we store and protect what you create using our services. This can include:

- Emails **that** you send and receive on Gmail

- Contacts **that** you add

- Calendar events

- Photos and videos **that** you upload

- Docs, Sheets, and Slides on Drive

Things that make you "you"

When you sign up for a Google account, we keep the basic information **that** you give us. This can include your:

- Name

- Email address and password

- Date of birth

- Gender

- Telephone number

- Country

(Google Data Privacy Policy, 2017)

Note the expressions "we collect data to make these services work for you" and "Things that make you "you", which basically translates to "the data we collect about you trains our algorithms to know you as much as possible about you."

Third Party Data

Let's now turn our attention to another type of data source **that is** feeding into Google, Facebook, Twitter, and other companies leveraging big data. That is companies purchasing data from third-party providers. Consider for example that in 2015 it was expected that almost 42 million smart wearable devices would be manufactured around the world, generating personal data about the subsequent wearers' fitness, sports activity, weight, body mass index, lean mass, body fat percentage, steps taken, floors climbed, distance walked/run, calorie intake, calories burned, active minutes a day, and sleep patterns. (Marr, 2015; Marr, 2016) And in 2016 it was expected that over a period of the next five years a further billion wearable devices would be produced. (Kelly, 2016) **Furthermore,** 3 billion appliances, such as the Nest Thermostat, are expected to find their way on to our cell phones, and 100 billion chips will be embedded into the goods on Walmart's shelves. (Kelly, 2016) Smart TVs count the number of people watching TV. (Marr, 2015) The 'Up' band created by Jawbone collects 60 years 's worth of sleep data every night and that data can be sold to interested third parties. (Marr, 2015) Mobile app Good2Go is being marketed as an "educational app for sexual consent", enabling couples to consent to sexual activity prior to the actual act. What couples are not aware of is that the company formulated its privacy in a way that allows them to sell data such as who you had sex with and at what time. Of course, they may choose not to do so but the point is that their policy clearly states that the company "may not be able to control how your personal information is treated, transferred or used". (Ross, 2017, p 176) Probably the biggest third party provider of data is a company called Acxiom, which claims to hold data on "all but a small percentage" of US households. (Marr, 2016) Acxion collects data from credit agencies about most US citizens, historical and current data of their domicile, how many children there are in their family, what magazines they subscribe to, public social media activity, public records such as electoral rolls, marriage and birth certificates, surveys completed, and much more. (Marr, 2015) I think we can agree that this is a lot of data, particularly when you consider that a credit rating agency such as Experian holds over 30 petabytes of information about people's credit history, age, location, and income status; and over 282 other credit rating attributes are measured to help financial companies in fraud detection. (Marr, 2015) Other examples of data sources include the now-defunct inBloom database sharing confidential student records with marketers, companies selling lists of families with illnesses such as AIDS or gonorrhea, lists of rape victims. (Ross, 2017)

We can now see that data companies such as Google develop your digital file by making their way into every area of your life, whether you're using your mobile device, watching TV, browsing the Internet, or heating your house. This takes us to the next point, which is that algorithms will soon be able to make sense of all this data and even end up by knowing you better than you know yourself. Harari proposes that humans are **nothing but** a collection of algorithms, and that an external algorithm could **in fact** learn to "manage" these algorithms better than we humans can. Many people may disagree, but Harari emphatically concludes that "attributing free will to humans is not an ethical judgment" (Harari, 2015, p. 283). **The idea that** humans are consciously making most of their decisions has been proven wrong **over and over again** by scientists and psychologists in thousands of experiments demonstrating that human decision-making sits mainly beyond our awareness. Genes and the environment work together behind the scenes, pulling the strings and determining every action we perform. We see ourselves as **being** in charge of our decisions, but we are puppets operated by forces outside our awareness. For the time being, consider this disturbing thought: if you are presented with a choice of two switches, simply by looking at your neural activity scientists can tell which switch you will press before you consciously **decide to** press it (Harari, 2015). Yes, your inner algorithms have **already** decided which switch you will press. So much for your free will and conscious decision-making. **In fact, researchers** implanted electrodes into the sensory and reward areas of rats' brains, then built a remote control system allowing them to control the movement of the rats. Simply press left, and a rat will turn left. Press another button and the rat climbs a ladder. **Keep in mind that** it all apparently happens beyond the level of consciousness of the rat, the rat does not think it is being controlled but **rather** feels a desire to turn left and it turns left (Harari, 2015). And an algorithm with sufficient information to know our inner workings will most often make **far better decisions than we** would make ourselves. And it would **certainly** make better recruitment decisions than we would do. Harari suggests that if we gave Google and its competitors access to our biometric devices, DNA information, medical records, fitness information, and so forth, their algorithms would prevent many of the bad decisions we humans make.

He concludes that:

> unlike the narrating self that controls us today, Google will not **make decisions on** the basis of cooked-up stories, and will not be misled by cognitive shortcuts. Google will actually remember every step we took …Google will advise us which movie to see, where to go on holiday, what to study in college, which job offer to accept, and even whom to date or marry.
>
> (Harari, 2015, p. 337)

If you believe this to be a sci-fi scenario, **you may want to** remember the study conducted by Facebook on 86,220 volunteers, which found that Facebook's algorithms only needed 10 likes performed by a user to judge their personality better than their work colleagues could, 70 likes for Facebook to know volunteers better than their friends did, 150 likes to know them better than family members did, and 300 likes to predict their opinions and desires better than their spouses could. The conclusion of the research was that humans would be better if they ceded important life decisions to algorithms (Harari, 2015)....recruitment is **one of those important decisions** too. Harari **goes as far as proposing** that we should replace the old "Listen to your feelings" dogma with a **completely** new one: "Listen to the algorithms! They know how you feel". (Harari, 2015, p 392) **In fact,** allowing a Google RankBrain-powered assistant to take over your everyday decisions and various important ones would make sense. **In the end, its** strong focus on user experience could only translate to a better life for you, the user. The idea is not new; Kelly, for example, describes filtering as one of the top digital trends of the future. (Kelly, 2016) To understand the importance of allowing Google to filter our choices, imagine yourself searching Amazon for a management book. I have just typed "management" in the books search bar and Amazon returned 1,326,652 books. **Given the fact that** our attention spans are **at present** as low as 8 seconds vs. 12 seconds in 2008 (Jones, 2014), and the massive increases in choices, lack of filtering could simply paralyze our ability to choose. **Thus, without** realizing it we have **already** ceded power to algorithms, and we trust that all the data we've fed into them over the years has trained them to make the right choices for us. On reflection, 95% of my Amazon book purchase choices are made via the recommendation system. You may not consciously realize but you have **already** ceded control to Google for many of your choices. Simply by typing a search query in Google's search box and clicking on one of its results you allow Google to decide what information is relevant for you. As Pedro Domingos puts it, " Google's algorithms largely determine what information you find…the last mile is still yours, choosing from the options the algorithm presents you with, but 99.9% of the selection was done for them". (Domingos, 2017, p 12) Still not convinced? Imagine Google altered its algorithms tomorrow, and all today's search results on first pages will be replaced with new results. The studies I presented clearly indicate that you would click almost exclusively on first page search results. Google has now chosen the content you read and influenced your opinions, and all with a simple tweak to its algorithms. So, how could this level of confidence in our smart assistants **look in the future**? Let's consider **a couple of** examples. Need to dress for an occasion? You may allow your personal assistant to scan your wardrobe, and pick the dress best matched to the profile of the person you are seeing. We are already ceding control to the algorithms in choosing the person we will spend our life with, if we are to consider the statistic that one-third of marriages in the US start with online dating (Ross, 2017). Similarly, forty percent of Americans use online dating and twenty percent of current committed relationships began online (Totham, 2017).

So, what will all these mean in the context of recruitment?

As we will cede more control to algorithms, algorithms will get to know us better than our friends, colleagues, spouses and even than we know ourselves. If you think about it, we already saw that algorithms can recognize and analyze your voice, recognize you in images, analyze text and so much more all over the internet: your social media profiles, your fridge, your TV watching habits, your mobile, what you read, how long you read etc. Thus, as you willingly hand over control to your personal assistant and other algorithms, these algorithms "know" you well: your strengths and weaknesses, your values, your habits and so forth. This has good and bad consequences for you. From a recruitment perspective, you cannot fool the algorithm; the algorithm will see beyond your overconfidence, attractiveness or CV, and will make no inappropriate inferences or associations between the unrelated traits or characteristics you possess...you cannot talk your way into a job. Conversely, an HR algorithm developed by companies as Google, Amazon, or Facebook will also build a digital profile of the company you have been applying to (i.e., employee surveys available in digital form, employee forums, corporate identity, customer feedback, etc.) and determine that your values do not match the company values, you will not enjoy the environment and you are better off searching elsewhere. The algorithm will also draw a list with companies that would be a good fit for you and are recruiting for a role that would fit you like a glove as well! Oh, yes...and the HR algorithms employed by the company will identify your digital profile as a perfect fit too. Given these perfect matches, why interview a candidate at all? Simply apply, let the algorithms review your profile and receive your contract within two minutes. Goodbye human recruiters!

1.3.2 Computational Power

We have been discussing the evolution of big data and how companies like Google use big data to gain knowledge about us and our behavior. However, the existence of powerful algorithms such as Google's Rankbrain would never have been made possible without Google's ability to store, process, and analyze large amounts of data, such as videos, emails, online behavior, social media activity, and photos. The rise of cloud computing and of computer power over time has provided Google with the ability to store and manipulate the large amounts of data that will eventually enable RankBrain to know you better than you are known by your colleagues, friends, relatives, and even yourself. To understand the growth of cloud computing, consider that the number of files stored on Microsoft's Azure cloud network grew from four trillion in 2012 to ten trillion in present time. (Marr, 2016) However, the power of big data resides not in **the amount of** data owned but in the ability to store and process that data, something that in 2012 President Obama acknowledged by including in his budget a $126 million fund to develop exascale computing. Intel set itself a target of achieving this by 2018. (Chace, 2015) For a more glaring example of the increase in computing power consider China's Tianhe-2 supercomputer which has 32,000 CPUs in 125 cabinets (Chace, 2015) or **the fact** that about 1,000 computers contribute to answering your every Google Search query in less than 0.2 seconds. (Marr, 2016) Another example underlining the importance of data handling capacity comes from Acxiom, the data collection company we encountered in the section on big data. The company's growth soared following a partnership with Citibank in 1983, at which point another issue occurred. According to Acxiom's founder, Charles Morgan, the challenge became managing growth and the lack of computing capacity. (Marr, 2016) Finally, if you are familiar with Moore's law, **you will not be surprised to hear that** the rule still holds true: every 18 months the computing power of microprocessors doubles. (Brynjolfsson & McAfee, 2016)

1.3.3 Advancements in AI

Google is getting smarter; that's what SEOs like to tell their clients **in an attempt** to keep the magic veil surrounding their profession. Google's RankBrain is often mentioned to imbue the search engine with an ability to learn in a similar way to the far more highly complex human brain. And Google's misleading name for its RankBrain algorithm does nothing to detract from the aura of humanness surrounding the learning and processing capabilities of RankBrain. Let's try to get this right and clarify the AI learning process that actually makes Google smarter. By understanding how it learns, we will better understand both the myths and the possible future capability of algorithms like RankBrain and of course of HR trained algorithms. We will also be in a far better position to judge the role of SEOs, and set the scene for understanding the future of human recruiters and the status of their profession. There are two main paths for algorithms like RankBrain to achieving AI status. Brain emulation is one path described by Bostrom (2016) for reaching human-level intelligence. So, will algorithms like RankBrain be able to achieve AI via this route? In principle, Bostrom points out that the problem is not necessarily knowing how to achieve this goal per se, but having the technology required to achieve it. Consider that your brain generates over a billion billion floating point operations per second. (Chace, 2015) The computing power needed to achieve this kind of performance is well beyond realistic achievements. For example, a team led by Markus Diesmann and Abigail Morrison has managed to create a neural network of 1.73 billion nerve cells, which were connected by 10.4 trillion synapses. This sounds impressive until we remember that a human brain contains 80 billion nerve cells. Diesmann and Morrison were able to simulate only one second of real brain activity. It took 82,944 processors and 1 PB of system memory to achieve this outcome. (Whitwam , 2013)

This attempt suggests that achieving AI by emulating the human brain is mission impossible. Instead of brain emulation, there are several technologies that could be used in trying to create a copy of the brain, 3D printing being the one most often mentioned. Another method involves sending nano-robots into a brain to survey neurons and return sufficient data to create a 3D map. (Chace, 2015) However, these technologies, like many others in the field, are well underdeveloped and incapable of coping with the complexity of the brain; none is considered a realistic means of emulating it. In addition to the matter of being able to map all the elements of the brain, there is the fact that all those elements continuously interact with each other with no specific pattern. This means that any scanning technology would also need to capture and replicate these interactions in real time. The truth is that most scientists in the field do not believe that human-level AI will first be achieved through brain emulation. Bostrom concludes: "the emulation path will not succeed in the near future (within the next fifteen years, say) because we know that several challenging precursor technologies have not yet been developed." (Bostrom, 2016, p. 43) Hence, thinking of algorithms as Google's RankBrain as a brain per se will not tell us much about the path Google will take to achieve its AI goals. We are left with the second path, which is machine learning. Machine learning is the process of creating algorithms that are able to gain insights from data fed into them without their being programmed to do so in detail. Recognizing lions in images, in spite of the image not being optimized is one example. As opposed to the human brain, which can quickly learn what a lion looks like, an algorithm needs to be fed with millions of images of lions to categorize what a lion is. Once it has acquired a concept of the characteristics of a lion, the algorithm will start a continuous process of trial and error, until it reaches a conclusion of what is and what is not a lion—what a lion looks like. Take an example of Google feeding its algorithms with millions of images of what it believes to be a lion. Google generated these images from various sources, including the alt text or optimization info provided by SEOs. Suppose you have optimized a Shutterstock image of a lion, while another webmaster has purchased the same image but done nothing to optimize it. RankBrain now monitors responses such as click-through rates, time on site, and so forth against user queries for lion images. Should the metrics indicate that your image does have a lion in it, the metrics will assume the same for the same un-optimized image. You now have an image that is being categorized by RankBrain as a lion in spite of having no alt tag or other optimization performed on it. Of course, this is a gross oversimplification. In fact, image recognition is becoming more and more a commodity, which is testimony to the advancements in this field. For example, Amazon's Rekognition service:

makes it easy to add image and video analysis to your applications. You just provide an image or video to the Rekognition API, and the service can identify the objects, people, text, scenes, and activities, **as well as** detect any inappropriate content. Amazon Rekognition also provides highly accurate facial analysis and facial recognition. You can detect, analyze, and compare faces for a wide variety of user verification, cataloging, people counting, and public safety use cases (Amazon Rekognition, 2018)

Machine learning is the path that RankBrain is most likely to take to achieve AI level. Algorithms have **in fact** already **managed to surpass** humans in many tasks requiring skills **that were** previously thought to be restricted to humans. Consider the well-publicized example of IBM Watson, which **managed to beat** the champions at the TV quiz game Jeopardy as early as 2011, and which is now being used in various industries, including as a business SAS model for AI. IBM Watson machine learning algorithms apply "more than 100 different techniques to analyze natural language, identify sources, find and generate hypotheses, find and score evidence, and merge and rank hypotheses". (Wikipedia, 2018) IBM Watson's "brain" is made of up of 90 IBM Power 750 servers processing 500 gigabytes of data per second (Marr, 2016), another example of improvements in computational power directly supporting advancements in the big data and machine learning fields. In fact, despite the deceiving name most so-called artificial intelligence entities currently employ machine learning technologies to achieve AI status. Further examples of AI outperforming humans include the CHINOOK algorithm drawing games with the checkers champion as early as 1994, Eurisko program winning the US championship in Traveler TCS (a futuristic naval war game), Deep Blue beating the reigning world chess champion in 1997 and many similar achievements, in crosswords and in games such as scrabble, bridge, poker, and go. (Bostrom, 2016) Just like IBM, and in spite of its deceiving RankBrain name, Google uses the machine learning path to achieve its AI goals. This is no secret, with Peter Norvig, director of research at Google, confirming in a chat with Pedro

Domingos that Google uses machine learning in literally everything it does (Domingos, 2017). Understanding this idea is essential in helping you to understand the end point and the effects of a fully developed RankBrain algorithm. To sum up, in spite of the human aura created by the "brain" association with its RankBrain algorithm, Google algorithms work nothing like a brain. Throughout the book, whenever I refer to AI capability, **keep in mind** I am referring to the machine learning arm of the AI field.

1.4 Time to cede control to Google

Kevin Kelly puts forward the very interesting idea of a future of leveraging the power of AI for improving and simplifying our increasingly complex and demanding lives. This idea made me think about an article I once read in which Facebook co-founder Mark Zuckerberg is asked his reason for wearing the same **type of** grey shirt every day. Zuckerberg's answer:

> I really want to clear my life so **that** I have to make **as few** decisions **as possible** about anything except how to best serve this community. I'm in this **really** lucky position where I get to wake up every day and help serve more than a billion people, and I feel like I'm not doing my job if I spend any of my energy on things that are silly or frivolous about my life, so **that** way I can dedicate all of my energy toward just building the best products and services

(Trotman, 2014)

Zuckerberg's answer provides a glimpse into the complexity and multitude of choices we will make **in the not too distant future**, although not all choices will be related to following our passions. Burdened with these choices, we will welcome any opportunity to simplify our lives and focus on things **that are** not being "silly or frivolous". But how will we achieve this? Yuval Noah Harari proposes that AI advancements will lead us to ceding control to intelligent assistants that will know us better than our colleagues, friends, or relatives do. (Harari, 2015) We have already spoken about the insights gained by algorithms into our character based on what we "like" on Facebook. Complementing Facebook's findings, another study performed at Cambridge University found that your Facebook likes enabled algorithms to better predict personal characteristics such as sexual orientation, satisfaction with life, intelligence, emotional stability, religion, alcohol use, relationship status, age, gender, race, and political views, and more. (Marr, 2015) You should not be surprised then to **find out** that Facebook's algorithms have improved to a degree where Facebook can now predict when you will change your relationship status from "single" to "in a relationship". (Marr, 2015) You can, I hope already see intuitively how algorithms **will be able to** make better recruitment decisions that humans. For example, the predictive single-in a relationship algorithm developed by Facebook may also predict that an employee is ready for another challenge. You could go even further: an algorithm performing sentiment analysis may identify that you are just about to **start searching** for another position (by analyzing your social media, performing sentiment analysis, monitoring changes in your behavior and habits). So the algorithm now knows the company will soon have a vacancy. And what does it do? Well it **starts looking** through the digital file of all potential internal and external candidates, identify potential candidates **which are** best fit to the company and to your job role, predict the likelihood **that** they would be available around the same time you **decide to** leave, contact them and send the contract on acceptance of the job – no human interaction **whatsoever**...goodbye HR interviewers, goodbye overpaid HR recruiters, goodbye bad employment decisions – hello perfect match between corporate identity – organizational identity – corporate image and reputation ! **In fact, online** dating websites such as eHarmony are already taking the guesswork and personal biases out of the profiling equation by profiling clients on about thirty particular attributes (Marr, 2015). I dare say that **in the near future,** your Google intelligent assistant will gain access to real-time information such as your heart rate, breathing rates, steps taken, and number of calories burned. It will hear who you talk to in a board meeting, analyze your voice and language, and determine your **appropriate** course of action. If you consider this to be a sci-fi scenario, the well-known fashion company Ralph Lauren has **already** been testing shirts that include devices that collect all the data I have just mentioned (Marr, 2016). Similarly, Squid, a smart shirt tested at Northeastern University in the USA **has the capability of determining** your posture and activating parts of the shirt to bring you to the optimal posture (Kelly, 2016). Google also funded project Jacquard, which included experiments with smart fabrics that both collect information and return information on a screen simply by swiping the sleeve of your shirt with your fingers.

Or take the example of Amazon, who patented a system called "anticipatory shipping" (Marr, 2015, p. 205). **In effect, the** patent underlines Amazon's belief in predicting and dispatching your purchases before you actually **made the decision** of buying it. So why not…a similar HR trained algorithm may **start looking** for your replacement before you actually **made a decision** of leaving. Still not convinced? Consider **the amount of** targeting options already available to advertisers via Facebook's Audience Insights platform. As an advertiser, you may **choose to** show your Facebook ad to people based on location, age, interests, connections, and more advanced options. Not very convincing, right? Things change when you drill down within the **various** categories. For example, the Interests category includes very granular targeting options such as interests in various industries (e.g. advertising, agriculture, banking), the entertainment you consume (e.g. type of movies, books you read, TV shows, music, games), family and relationships (e.g. dating, family make-up, fatherhood, friendship, marriage, parenting), fitness and wellness (e.g. bodybuilding, dieting, gym membership, meditation, nutrition, yoga). You can **choose to** deliver your ads to people based on their behavior, language, relationship status, education, work, financial situation, home type and value, parents, politics, life events, and much more. Yes, I can deliver my ad to single dads with two children, MBA educated, earning over £75,000, owning a £500,000 house, who practice yoga, have certain political views, and so forth. This is all being made possible because Facebook already has this information about you. **After all, remember** that over 25% of us do not even bother with any **kind of** privacy settings!

Perhaps the Cambridge Analytica scandal of 2018 best indicates the amount of data about us that companies like Facebook have in their possession. Aleksandr Kogan, Cambridge Analytica's chief researcher was reportedly proud of scraping the Facebook profiles of "50+ million individuals for whom we have the capacity to predict virtually any trait." (Romano, 2018) Most people, and public opinion condemned this mischievous act of harvesting our personal data, ignoring the reality that WE provided access to our data by mismanagement of our privacy settings and by uploading massive amounts of information to our Facebook profiles, adding to it daily. As Aja Romano concludes: "The Facebook data breach wasn't a hack. It was a wake-up call." (Romano, 2018)

The examples could continue; however, **the point is that** algorithms will have so much data about you **that** they will succeed in monitoring you right down to some psychological levels you have little access to consciously, well below your level of awareness. Yes, I am saying that the algorithm will get to know you better than you know yourself. To recap: improvements in AI, particularly in its arm of machine learning will enable algorithms such as Google or Facebook's to better assess the fit between the potential employee and the company while also reducing reliance on traditional "ranking" factors i.e. gut instinct **which have been** shown to be highly inefficient following my study of managers and HR professionals.

Given the depth of information held about you, AI algorithms may take a more in-depth approach to analyzing the cultural fit between a candidate and an organization. Past information collected within your digital file will be complemented by real-time information about your behavior and state of mind. While gazing at your Google Pixel phone, the device will gaze back at you, classify your state of mind, and analyze your reactions and feelings throughout the interview, if there will ever be one. The role of the interviewers will be reduced to ask a predefined set of questions, and no input will be required of them in terms of the actual decision of employment – the deskilling of recruiters will be reflected in lower wages and status. The interview will be recorded and later analyzed by various algorithms that will make the final decision on the person employed – no emotions, no biases, no overconfident or incompetent bosses: just a pure culture of meritocracy.

If that sounds too futuristic for you, consider some of the technology already available, thanks to the efforts of Rosalind Picard and Rana el Kaliouby, two MIT researchers who developed software capable of detecting human emotions via smartphone camera devices. The software can identify whether you are depressed, perplexed, bored, or experiencing some other emotion while gazing at the phone (Kelly, 2016). Or, consider the machine learning service offered by Amazon's AWS DeepLens which "lets you run deep learning models locally on the camera to analyse and take action on what it sees". (AWSDeepLens, 2018) Yes, you heard me—the AWS camera, looking at you, analyses your environment and builds algorithms based on the goals you are setting up. Similarly, Amazon Reckognition will find you in the crowd, access your digital file and perform sentiment analysis on your face. On one side, this means no more hiding and no more deceiving for candidates. And it also means no more bad decisions made by the overly-biased HR professional or manager. The winner is, you guessed it... a consistent Corporate Identity promoted and adhered to almost fanatically by employees (organizational identity), which will deliver a corporate image and reputation consistent with the corporate identity.

Agreed, algorithms are not quite there yet. For example, in a search engine optimization context quality backlinks, content, and RankBrain represent the main signals contributing to ranking an website. However, make no mistake:

Google will gradually reduce the importance of backlinks or keywords as ranking factors, to the point where backlinks or keywords will play very little or no impact on ranking an website. This is almost a repeat of the past; it closely resembles the dismissal of factors such as meta descriptions, URLs, H1s, or page titles. If you have no knowledge of the terminology described above, do not worry – the point I am making is that performance of algorithms evolved to a point where humans already find it extremely hard to influence, let alone beat the significantly improved machine learning algorithms. In fact, the improvement of algorithms, whether SEO or recruitment related is an ongoing mechanism in the AI evolutionary process. Bostrom's explanation of the general AI process offers a very vivid understanding of the progress of algorithms such as Google's, from reliance on human input to its launch of and subsequent dependence on RankBrain. Bostrom explains that in the early stages of AI, improvements may occur through a trial-and-error process, acquiring data and assistance from programmers- in a recruitment environment that would be the human recruiters. However, at later stages the system should be able to improve and learn ways of working to the point that it will self-improve with no human input. This means that it could create new algorithms and structures boosting its cognitive performance. Furthermore, the system will be able to apply "recursive self-improvement, which means that it could improve or create a better version of itself, which then creates a better version, and so forth". (Bostrom, 2016, p.34) Or, in the words of Pedro Domingos: "...the more data they have the better they get. Now we don't have to program computers; they program themselves". (Domingos, 2017, p. xi) In a nutshell, any professional with recruitment responsibilities is naïve and guilty of wishful thinking if he or she expects to still maintain a role in employing people when algorithms such as RankBrain developed into a fully reliable AI "brain". If you have any doubts about where the future lies, let us revisit Larry Page's 2003 statement regarding the future of search: "Google will fulfill its mission only when its search engine is AI-complete...That's artificial intelligence". (Chace, 2015, p 18)

Many recruiters may try to dismiss the "algorithm only" outcome I foresee. As humans we **have the tendency to normalize** advancement in technology and take innovation for granted. **Indeed, over** time we have experienced great advancements in technology, such as smartphones, hearing aids with algorithms filtering out noise, systems offering product recommendations, speech recognition software, machine translation programs, and much more. And yet, we soon consider these advancements to be the norm, and pay little attention to what they represent, which in reality is a great improvement in AI technologies. Yes, given the smooth transition from one technology to another, we soon forget that change happens right here, **right now,** right in front of us. **Indeed, innovation** is work in progress and it **certainly** is not a one big aha moment. To make this point, I particularly like to quote Walton's statement in his Made in America biography: "…some folks have gotten the impression that…it was just this great idea that turned into an overnight success…And like most overnight successes, it was about twenty years in the making". (Walton & Huey, p. 35) In this context, **you can be sure that** Google is well on track to becoming an AI entity, and when that happens its business model will become "Take X and apply AI". (Kelly, 2014) **Of course,** in our case, this statement will become "Take recruitment, apply AI to HR, remove human recruiters from equation and make the right decisions both for the candidate and for the company".

Again, we are not quite there, however as Walton emphasized, his Wal-Mart achievement has not occurred in a big aha moment, but rather through the gradual accumulation of smaller and bigger innovations. Kelly named this continuous flow of change "a state of becoming", and pointed out that "unceasing change can blind us to its incremental change…we tend to see new things from the frame of old". (Kelly, 2016, p. 14) To remind myself about this point, I always find it useful to think about a situation described by Chace (2015). You are in a stadium. One drop of water is being dropped on to the pitch and then doubles every 60 seconds: 2 drops, 4 drops, 8 innovations, 16 innovations, 32 innovations, and so forth. You **may or may not** feel surprised to **find out** that it takes only 49 minutes to fill the stadium. What should surprise you though is that after 45 minutes the stadium is 93% empty of water hence the real progress occurs only within the last 4 minutes. And, to conclude my argument consider the following statement from Elon Musk: "The pace of progress in artificial intelligence is incredibly fast. Unless you have direct exposure to groups like Deepmind, you have no idea how fast—it is growing at a pace close to exponential…This is not a case of crying wolf about something I don't understand". (Chace, 2015, p. 89) Oh, and one more thing: Google has bought DeepMind for half a billion dollars (Domingos, 2017).

A more important idea, though, is that **in the future** you may not **be able to** buy paid ads, taxi rides, human recruiters or other similar **products at all.** Futurologist David Kelly suggests that by 2026 Google will not be in the paid search **business at all.** Kelly argues that "by 2026 Google's main product will not be searched but AI" and quotes Sundar Pichai, Google CEO, who **referred to AI as** " a core transformative way by which we are re-thinking everything we are doing…we are applying it across all our products, be it Search, YouTube and Play etc.". (Kelly, 2016, p. 37) Hence, **you should not be surprised** to learn that Google's core business will most likely gradually come to consist of supplying AI through the meter, **in the same way, energy companies** supply electricity. Kelly, in fact, takes the idea further and proposes that by 2025 most businesses will operate on a model of "Take X and apply AI," (Kelly, 2014)

But **surely,** you will argue - algorithms can never compensate for quality and traits specific to humans only, i.e., emotional intelligence, creativity, etc. To debunk these myths let me start by emphasizing that emotional intelligence (the ability to put yourself in someone else's shoes) is detrimental to an unbiased process of recruitment. We discussed the impact of inferring characteristics of candidates from unrelated characteristics, familiarity, similarity and so forth.

How about creativity? Well, progress has **already** been made in many areas we believed to be the reserve of human creativity. Some human input will most likely still be required in creative processes; however, these positions for humans will be very few and only open to the **very** best people. Most of us believe creativity is the reserve of the human species, consider it our competitive advantage, and argue passionately against signs which indicate **that** this may not be **quite** true. But, as one example of such signs, in 2012 the London Symphony Orchestra performed a piece named *Transits to an Abyss*, which was written by Iamus, and, as you may have **already** guessed, Iamus is an AI algorithm. Similarly, in his research on machines' ability to innovate, Stanford professor John Koza found that across **a variety of industries algorithms** produced designs competitive with work produced by humans. **Moreover, on** two occasions the work produced by algorithms created new patentable inventions. (Ford, 2016) Ok, you may continue to argue, but these algorithms **will never be able to** replicate human emotions **that are** so essential to the originality of a piece of art. However, we have **already** seen how technologies developed the ability to accurately identify human emotions at a deeper level than we perceive them ourselves consciously. The only challenge left for algorithms is getting the creative desire simulated and translate that into art. Again we are not quite there. However, some progress has been made in this direction. For example, Simon Colton of the University of London has created software that can accurately read emotions in photographs of people and paint abstract portraits that convey their emotional state. Hence the idea that creativity is an exclusively human attribute is a fallacy; algorithms such as RankBrain will prove us wrong.

This scenario is by no means a sci-fi fantasy, all you need do is again reflect on that co-founder's statement of Google's AI mission. On reflection, Google, Microsoft, and Amazon are already selling machine learning through the meter, via their Google Cloud, Microsoft Azure, and Amazon AWS platforms. For example, Amazon is already offering machine-powered capabilities to find relationships and insights within text (Amazon Comprehend), convert speech to text and build conversational applications (Amazon Lex), convert text to speech (Amazon Polly), recognize and analyze images and videos (Amazon Rekognition), translate text (Amazon Translate), and transcribe audio documents to text (Amazon Transcribe), while AWS DeepLens enables developers to run deep learning models locally on a camera, analyze their environment, perform sentiment analysis and build algorithms in line with their goals. (Amazon Comprehend, 2018)

This leads to the simple conclusion that Google's main revenue stream **in the future** will be AI and not paid ads. **In fact, paid** search will be reduced to one of many streams of revenue generated by Google. Following this line of thought, Google's core business will include leveraging AI capabilities to dominate traditional industries **that are** currently well out of its reach. The automotive industry is one example; Google's driverless car project is well known to most people with an **interest in the future**.

And why stop there? Why not Human Resources Algorithms – both for recruiting and for motivating people? As we saw already, Kevin Kelly made the very interesting prediction that the next 10,000 startups will in some shape or form employ a business model of "Take X and apply AI" (Chace, 2015). If Kelly is correct, companies could **end up having** to acquire AI units to power-up their Google-produced HR algorithm, reduce operational costs by making the HR function redundant altogether, and enhance corporate identity success by bringing the right people on board. You may stubbornly argue that companies will always need an HR person or as a minimum, a manager trained in HR tasks. I will not disagree; however, these positions will require little experience or specialized skills. Employees will only perform low-level administrative tasks, and the person will not **need** to be HR trained either. Just as I argued **in the case of** professional SEOs, the bargaining position will now move from experienced HR professionals to corporations, and this will be reflected in a lower renumeration and loss of status, in line with the low level of skills required to perform the job.

To conclude this section, in the long term, any form of human input in recruitment will be made redundant, with HR trained algorithms becoming the only HR professional organizations will ever need. The improvements in recruitment decisions will reflect in a better fit between the corporate identity and employee perceptions of it (organizational identity). Stakeholders, i.e., clients or employees in other organizations, etc., will also experience the corporate identity promoted by the company as real, tangible and genuine. This will build a corporate image and ultimately a corporate reputation consistent with the corporate identity promoted by the organization. Productivity will increase, and profits will grow as well (loss of human HR-related jobs, deskilling of managers and HR professionals). It's easy to identify the only **loser in this situation**, yes, it's you, the manager or HR professional, that used to have recruitment responsibility.

1.5 A trend to keep your eyes on

Ford (2016) identified a very important trend that brings us one step closer to understanding the process that will ultimately lead to the dismissal of human recruiters. This trend features two important aspects of the process leading to automation of human tasks. The obvious one is that jobs created via offshoring are temporary, and represent only a transitional step toward automation. The second aspect, though, is that while not ready to take on humans fully in some industries, algorithms enable the offshoring **relevant** jobs through the "automation funnel". McAfee and Brynjolfsson looked at the tasks that have been offshored within the previous 20 years and discovered **that** those tasks were routine, well-structured tasks that were the easiest to automate. McAfee concludes: "in other words, offshoring is often only a way station on the road to automation." (McAfee & Brynjolfsson, 2016, p. 184) As for the profession of human recruiter- whether a manager, supervisor or HR professional, the decline has started if you consider the variety of outsourcing services offering HR services at far lower costs than employing the services of HR professionals directly. For example, in one group of hotels I worked for, the HR function was outsourced to a specialized company at a lower cost. And even these services are starting to be made redundant by many HR Management online platforms that given the low fixed costs can offer HR services at a ridiculously low cost. Simply type HR management platform into Google and you will be amazed at the variety of such platforms.

1.6 VR & Augmented Reality

Kevin Kelly went to great lengths in reviewing the most disruptive technological platforms that **will impact** us within our **current** lifespan. He **referred to computers as** the first disruption, mobile phones as the second, and concluded: "the next disrupting platform now arriving is VR."(Kelly, 2016, p. 231) VR and augmented reality represent great HR opportunities that will not go unnoticed by companies **that are** looking to improve their employee-corporate identity fit by reducing the impact of human biases. As a candidate, you will wear your smart Google Glass everywhere you go, whether running, walking, driving, or having a coffee in your local coffee shop. Glass, powered by RankBrain will greatly enhance your productivity. You will simultaneously have your coffee, watch a movie, read a book, or read your emails. **Of course, many** other uses will make Google Glass an indispensable part of your wardrobe. Obviously, Google will apply AI technology to developing this new stream of revenue. As I mentioned earlier in the book, Glass will watch you, accurately identify your mood, your likes, and dislikes, where you look and for how long you do so, what you click on and what do after and so forth. Yes, Google is now monitoring every action you take while wearing Glass: what games you play, what movies you watch, what books you read, the meetings planned on your calendar, and even your attention span during a movie, book, or game. In a nutshell, given the digital form of VR technologies, every move you make is monitored, analyzed, and **further** used to build your Google digital file. Some data **that is** already being collected and analyzed via VR includes eye tracking, body motion, sound, data input, heartbeat, head movement, control inputs, communications, and much more. VR analytics will provide valuable information, given the findings of a Stanford University study that people behave **very** similarly in VR to how they do in real life (Sky, 2015). Given that you have ceded control to Google Assistant, algorithms will most likely know you better than you know yourself, further refining their understanding of "you".

But how will it look in practice?

You may be watching a movie and be shown an ad promoting a future vacancy. The algorithm predicted that the vacancy will be available within the next two months and you will be a perfect fit for it. In terms of augmented reality, while driving your car, ads are being shown as overlays on buildings throughout your journey, promoting the vacancy above. Augmented ads are personalized to your **current** mood, the time you spend in traffic, your earlier behavior, and so forth. The algorithm will not send you an ad about the organization if you are in a bad mood...you may unconsciously transfer that feeling to the organization. So, while looking at the very same landscape, the driver behind is being served different augmented ads, personalized to his own characteristics, mood, and digital profile. And if the HR algorithm thinks you may be the best candidate of them all, it may tailor the "sales" funnel to make you familiar with the company first. As we saw, familiarity breeds liking. While in traffic the augmented ad may show an ad promoting the values of the organization. You will like that, they match with yours like a glove. Back in your office, an ad is being shown on your Google Glass announcing the great plans for the future of the company that would like to employ you. On your coffee break, another ad, this time on your mobile announcing a predicted vacancy within the next two months. By now, you already know you must apply. You run the company and position through your HR algorithm – perfect match. You apply, the algorithm takes about a minute to process your digital profile, concludes you are the perfect match, sends the contract. You click the accept job button and that is it.

There is, however, one action that organizations can take right now to improve the efficiency of the recruitment process by limiting the damage of the human biases we have been discussing: replace face-to-face interviews with VR interviews. In this situation, all candidates will check in with the same avatar and communicate with the same voice. As discussed, given the digital format of the conversation, the interview can be analyzed against many factors. A sentiment analysis can be carried out, downloaded in a text format and sent to companies such as Narrative Science for generating reports and insights from within the text document it within a report format. This change will improve decision making by removing many biases we have been discussing: attractiveness of candidate, first impressions, stereotypes, intuition, misleading body language to name just a few.

Finally, as smart assistants establish themselves as the de facto "connector" of your household appliances, augmented paid ads will **start following** you around the house, knowing when you switch on your TV, open the fridge, or adjust your thermostat. **Indeed, consider** the estimation that between 2015 and 2020 the number of wirelessly connected devices will grow from 16 billion to 40 billion. Similarly, a report by Juniper estimated that smart home services will reach a global market value of $71 billion by 2025. Yes, the internet of things (IOT) will represent yet another advertising opportunity for the likes of Google and Facebook, and not a small **one I must say**. Google is already working hard on leveraging this opportunity and encouraging people to connect their smart houses through various Google products, such as Google Home, Google Home Mini, Google Wifi, Chromecast, Chromecast Audio, Nest Learning Thermostat, Nest Protect, Nest Cam IQ Indoor, Nest Cam indoor, and Nest Cam

Outdoor. Yes, Google is making it **as** easy **as possible** for you to digitize your life. Incidentally, this also allows its algorithms to continuously build your digital profile. Google will become the biggest corporation on the planet, their algorithms will be used in literally every industry on Earth including HR- the alternative to not using HR algorithms for your recruitment will represent commercial suicide. But then the same goes for Amazon, Microsoft, and Facebook. And who knows what other innovative companies may enter the game?

PART 4.

RECOMMENDATIONS FOR FURTHER RESEARCH

1.0 Corporate Identity Study

Several ideas must represent the subject of future research.

As age and length of service were found not to impact employee perceptions of corporate identity (as opposed to previous studies), it would be interesting to conduct the research on a larger sample of employees.

As it was found that corporate image, organizational image or corporate reputation have a low potential of affecting employee perceptions and commitment, the relationship between these factors and organizational identity must be studied further. As there was not sufficient data for a more detailed analysis, it would be interesting to study the impact of the organizational image-organizational identity gap on the corporate-organizational identity gap. Some employees stated that corporate image influenced their perceptions of Brand, and given the corporate image-organizational identity link, it should be further studied whether employees' perceptions were conditioned by perceptions of organizational identity, therefore if corporate image alone affects employee perceptions of brands.

An employee stated that his perception of Brand was not influenced by bi-polar views of Brand vs. Competitor because, based on its reputation, Competitor was a five-star chain and it was expected that it was better than Brand, which was rated as a four-star hotel chain. However, this perception raises a few other questions: If the employee was aware of Competitor's four stars rating within the UK, yet still perceived it as better than Brand, would this affect his perceptions about Brand and its positioning as a four-star chain? Or, if he was aware that Competitor's reputation was contradicted by a different identity in the UK, would this affect his perceptions of Competitor's corporate identity? And how would it affect his perception of Brand's identity? Thus, the link between corporate reputation-discrepant corporate identities-employee perceptions/commitment must be studied further.

One employee observed large gaps between cultures and recruitment strategies within her country and the UK culture. As the employee did not work for Brand in her country, a future study of a Brand hotel within her country would provide valuable information regarding the impact of national culture on corporate identity, and enhance our understanding of how corporate structure and growth strategy affected corporate identity.

However, the largest weakness of both my and of previous studies is the incomplete method of research. Specifically, both my and previous research are using self-reporting techniques, whether interviews, surveys or secondary data as company employee surveys. However, as I prompted in the section on Recommendations, we all fall prey to the mistaken belief that we can access our conscious mind, understand how it works, and decide freely. In reality though, as psychologist Claude M Steele points out earlier, "One of the first things one learns as a social psychologist is that everyone is capable of bias. We simply are not, and cannot be…completely objective." (Steele, 2011, p. 13) Hence a significant opportunity exists to research relationships between the many facets and factors influencing corporate identity using methods borrowed from social psychology studies. The relationships and findings of previous studies must be complemented by rigorous experiments, testing perceptions of employees beyond their own awareness. A comparison and analysis of the results of self-reporting methods vs. experiments will be carried out, and organizations will be in a better position of taking the correct actions in tackling the corporate identity – organizational identity gap.

1.1 Recruitment Study

Several ideas must represent the subject of future research:

Given the small sample and the reduced scope of my research, all findings on human biases in recruitment must be studied in greater detail.

A scientific approach to the study is recommended i.e. experiments - as opposed to asking managers about their **awareness of** factors such as attractiveness of candidate, mood, age of recruiter, etc., and how it affected their decisions (potentially leading them to an answer or to consider factors they may not have been considering in a real-life situation), experiments must reveal managers' actual levels of awareness, knowledge, perceptions and practices. Obviously, this approach would require **large resources** such as time, money, participants, academic environment, etc. The research must be extended to investigate the perceptions and levels of knowledge within the management academia as well. Specifically, are teachers, lecturers or professors of management equipped with the knowledge to teach, train, and develop leaders and managers in relation to the factors discussed?

Collins (74:2001) found that "expending energy trying to motivate people is largely a waste of time…if you have the right people on the bus they will be self-motivated". Thus, motivating people must also be thought of and studied as a function of marketing rather than as a HR tool. Indeed, many scientific studies confirm that traditional motivational practices affect employee efficiency and adoption of corporate identity. **For example, in many companies, employees are largely motivated with financial awards and commissions** (Kahneman, 75:2011). **However, numerous experiments confirmed that** "this system destroys the interest of the work in the eye of the employee" (Kahneman, 78:2011), "people will engage less in the activity after the reward is withdrawn than people who have never been rewarded" (Kahneman, 75:2011), employees lost intrinsic motivation for the task (Deci in Pink, 8:2009) and "by offering a reward, a principal signals that the task is undesirable" (Pink, 54:2009). **Thus, it is likely that** once on board, the right people can be demotivated, lose interest in the job, and reduce their intrinsic commitment to brand identity, with an implicit impact on brand's perceptions by external stakeholders (i.e. corporate image, corporate reputation). As Collins argues, a more important question **needs asking**: "How do you manage in such a way not to de-motivate people?" **Management academics must** focus on providing answers to this question, and employ methods of research from traditional management (i.e., interviews, surveys, etc.) and social psychology (i.e. experiments).

REFERENCES AND FURTHER READINGS

[1] Anon (2003), Longman: Dictionary of Contemporary English, Pearson Education Limited

[2] Anon (2017), *More Than Half of HR Managers Say Artificial Intelligence Will Become a Regular Part of HR in Next 5 Years*, Retrieved from http://press.careerbuilder.com/2017-05-18-More-Than-Half-of-HR-Managers-Say-Artificial-Intelligence-Will-Become-a-Regular-Part-of-HR-in-Next-5-Years

[3] Anon (2016), *Global Recruiting Trends 2016*, Retrieved at https://business.linkedin.com/content/dam/business/talent-solutions/global/en_us/c/pdfs/GRT16_GlobalRecruiting_100815.pdf

[4] Anon (2018), *HR Data Difficulties*, Retrieved at https://www.sdworx.com/en-us/press/2018-06-06-hr-data-difficulties

[5] Amazon Comprehend (2018). Amazon Comprehend. Discover Insights and relationships in text, Retrieved from https://aws.amazon.com/comprehend/?nc2=h_a1

[6] Amazon Lex (2018), *Amazon Lex. Conversational Interfaces for Your Applications. Powered by the same deep learning technologies as Alexa*, Retrieved at https://aws.amazon.com/lex/?nc2=h_a1

[7] Amazon Rekognition (2018), *Deep learning-based image and video analysis*, Retrieved from https://aws.amazon.com/rekognition/?nc2=h_a1

[8] AWS DeepLens (2018), *The world's first deep learning enabled video camera for developers*, Retrieved at https://aws.amazon.com/deeplens/?nc2=h_m1

[9] Anderson, Chris (2009). *The Longer Tail. How Endless choice is creating unlimited demand*, GB: Random House Business Books

[10] Anon, *Assessing ethical issues*,
URL: http://www.resmind.swap.ac.uk/content/07_being_a/being_a_06.htm

[22 Dec 2008]

[11] Appleton, Adam (2017), *The Machine Learning and AI Recruiting Future*, Retrieved at https://recruiterswebsites.com/ai-recruiting-future/

[12] Ariely, Dan (2008), *Predictability Irrational*, Harper Collins Publishers

[13] Balmer, M.T. John (2008), *Identity based views of the corporation: Insights from corporate identity, organizational identity, social identity, visual identity, corporate brand identity and corporate image*; European Journal of Marketing, vol 42 no 9/10, Emerald Group Publishing Limited

[14] Balmer, M.T. John and Greyser, A Stephen (2006), *Corporate marketing: Integrating corporate identity, corporate branding, corporate communications, corporate image and corporate reputation*, European Journal of Marketing, vol 40 no 7/8, pg 730-741, Emerald Group Publishing Limited

[15] Balmer, MT John and Gray, R Edmund (2000), *Corporate identity and corporate communications: creating a competitive advantage*, Industrial and Commercial Training, vol 32 no 7, pg 256-261, MCB UP

[16] Baker, J Michael, and Balmer, M.T. John (1997), *Visual identity: trappings or substance?*, European Journal of Marketing, vol 31 no 5/6, pg 366-382, MCB UP

[17] Barnatt, Christopher (2013). *3D Printing. The Next Industrial Revolution*, GB: ExplainingTheFuture.com

[18] Beamery (2018), *Treat Candidates Like Customers*, Retrieved at https://beamery.com/

[19] Bernstein, David (2009), *Rhetoric and reputation: some thoughts on corporate dissonance*, Management Decision, vol 47 no 4, pg 603-615, Emerald Group Publishing Limited

[20] Bloom, Paul (2010), *How Pleasure Works: Why we like what we like*, The Bodley Head Vintage

[21] Bostrom, Nick (2016). *Superintelligence. Paths, Dangers, Strategies*, GB: Oxford University Press

[22] Bowen, T John, and Chen, Shiang-Lih (2001), *The relationship between customer loyalty and customer satisfaction*, International Journal of Contemporary Hospitality Management, vol 13 no 5, pg 213-217, MCB UP

[23] Bronn, Peggy Simcic; Engell, Andreas, and Martinsen, Havard (2006), *A reflective approach to uncovering actual identity*, European Journal of Marketing, vol 40 no 7/8, pg 886-901, Emerald Group Publishing Limited

[24] Brynjolfsson, Erik & McAfee, Andrew (2016). *The Second Machine Age. Work, Progress, And Prosperity in a Time of Brilliant Technologies*, US: Norton

[25] Chabris, Christopher & Simons, Daniel (2010). *The Invisible Gorilla And Other Ways Our Intuition Deceives Us*, GB: Harper Collins Publishers

[26] Chace, Calum (2015). *Surviving AI. The promise and peril of artificial intelligence*, GB: Three Cs

[27] Collins, Jim (2001), *Good to Great*, Random House Business Books

[28] Cornelissen, Joep (2000), *Corporate image: an audience centred model*, Corporate Communications: An International Journal, vol 5 no 2, pg 119-125, MCB UP

[29] Cornelissen, P Joep, and Elving, JL Wim (2003), *Managing corporate identity: an integrative framework of dimensions and determinants*, Corporate Communications: An International Journal, vol 8 no 2, pg 114-120, MCB UP

[30] Coleman, David (2018), *How Bots Are Streamlining the HR Recruitment Process*, retrieved at https://www.cmswire.com/digital-workplace/how-bots-are-streamlining-the-hr-recruitment-process/

[31] Dalio, Ray (2017), Ted Talk retrieved at https://www.youtube.com/watch?time_continue=715&v=HXbsVbFAczg

[32] de Chernatony, Leslie and Cottam, Susan (2008), *Interactions between organizational cultures and corporate brands*, Journal of Product & Brand Management, vol 17 no 1, pg 13-24, Emerald Group Publishing Limited

[33] Dickson, Ben (2017), *How artificial intelligence optimizes recruitment*, Retrieved at https://thenextweb.com/contributors/2017/06/03/artificial-intelligence-optimizes-recruitment-hiring/

[34] Domingos, Pedro (2017). *The Master Algorithm. How The Quest For The Ultimate Learning Machine Will Remake Our World*, UK: Penguin Books

[35] Duhigg, Charles (2012). *The Power of Habit. Why we do what we do and how to change*, UK: Random House

[36] Dweck, S. Carol (2007), *Mindset*, The Random House Publishing Group

[37] Enge, Eric. Spencer, Stephan. Stricchiola, Jessie & Fishkin, Rand (2013). *The Art of SEO. Mastering Search Engine Optimization*, US: O'Reilly

[38] Ford, Martin (2016). *The Rise of the Robots*, GB: Oneworld Publications

[39] Frei, Frances and Moriss, Anne (2012), *Uncommon Service: How to Win by Putting Customers at the Core of your Business*, Harvard Business Review Press

[40] Next Tech Magazine (2017). *Google Tips & Tricks. Unlock the power of the world's most amazing free apps*, UK: Future Publishing Ltd

[41] Gardner, Dan (2009). *Risk. The Science and Politics of Fear*, GB: Virgin Books

[42] Gilbert, Daniel (2007), *Stumbling on Happiness*, HarperCollins Publishers

[43] Gill, S. Amarjit (2008), *The role of trust in employee-manager relationship*, International Journal of Contemporary Management, vol 20 no 1, pg 98-103, Emerald Group Publishing Limited

[44] Godin, Seth (2005). *Purple Cow. Transform Your Business by Being Remarkable*, UK: Penguin Business

[45] Godin, Seth (2012). *All Marketers Are Liars*, US: Penguin Books

[46] Google (2017), *Google Products*, retrieved from https://www.google.com/intl/en/about/products

[47] Google (2017), *Data Privacy Policy*, Retrieved from https://privacy.google.com/intl/en-GB/your-data.html

[48] Gotsi, Manto; Andriopoulus, Constantine and Wilson, Alan (2008), *Corporate re-branding: is cultural alignment the weakest link?* Management Decision, vol 46 no 1, pg 46-57, Emerald Group Publishing Limited

[49] Gotsi, Manto and Adriopoulos, Constantine (2007), *Understanding the pitfalls in the corporate re-branding process*, Corporate Communications: An International Journal, vol 12 no 4, pg 341-355

[50] Goyal, Malini (2017), *How artificial intelligence is reshaping recruitment, and what it means for the future of jobs*, Retrieved at https://economictimes.indiatimes.com/jobs/how-artificial-intelligence-is-reshaping-recruitment-and-what-it-means-for-the-future-of-jobs/articleshow/60985946.cms

[42] Hai-yan, Kong and Baum, Tom (2006), *Skills and work in the hospitality sector: The case of hotel front office employees in China*, International Journal of Contemporary Hospitality Management, vol 18 no 6, pg 509-518

[43] Haktanir, Mine and Harris, Peter (2005), *Performance measurement practice in an independent hotel context: A case study approach*, International

Journal of Contemporary Hospitality Management, vol 17 no 1, pg 39-50, Emerald Group Publishing Limited

[44] Hallier, Jerry, and Leopold, John (1996), *Creating and replicating HRM on greenfield sites: rhetoric or reality?*, Employee Relations, vol 18 no 5, pg 46-65, MCB UP

[45] Harari, Yuval Noah (2015). *Homo Deus. A Brief History of Tomorrow*, GB: Harvill Secker

[46] Harris, Fiona and de Chernatony, Leslie (2001), Corporate branding and corporate brand performance, European Journal of Marketing, vol 35 no 3/4, pg 441-456, MCB UP

[47] Hatch, Jo Mary and Schultz, Majken (1997), *Relations between organizational culture, identity and image*, European Journal of Marketing, vol 31 no 5/6, pg 356-365, MCB UP

[48] He, Wong-Wei and Balmer, MT John (2007), *Identity studies: multiple perspectives and implications for corporate-level marketing*, European Journal of Marketing, vol 41 no 7/8, pg 765-785, Emerald Group Publishing Limited

[49] Herstein, Ram; Mitki, Yoram and Jaffe D. Eugene (2007), *From Blueprint to implementation: Communicating corporate identity for the hotel industry*, International Journal of Contemporary Hospitality Management, vol 19 no 6, pg 485-494, Emerald Group Publishing Limited

[50] Holtzhausen, Lida and Fourie, Lynnette (2008), *Communicate to a diverse workforce. Employee perceptions of symbolic corporate identity elements*, Corporate Communications: An International Journal, vol 13 no 1, pg 80-94, Emerald Group Publishing Limited

[51] Hood, Bruce (2009). *Supersense. From Superstition to Religion- the Brain Science of Belief*, GB: HarperCollins Publishers

[52] ideal.com (2018), *AI For Recruiting: A Definitive Guide For HR Professionals,* Retrieved at https://ideal.com/ai-recruiting/

[53] Iverson, D Roderick; McLeod, S Colin and Erwin, J Peter (1996), *The role of employee commitment and trust in service relationships*, Marketing Intelligence & Planning, vol 14 no 3, pg 36-44, MCB UP

[54] Johnson, Rick (2008), *Do as I say- Not as I do!*

URL: http://www.4hoteliers.com/4hots_fshw.php?mwi=3475

[19 Nov 2008]

[55] Josh Bersin, Laurence Collins, David Mallon, Jeff Moir, Robert Straub (2016), *People analytics -*

Gaining speed, Retrieved at https://www2.deloitte.com/insights/us/en/focus/human-capital-trends/2016/people-analytics-in-hr-analytics-teams.html

[56] Kahneman, Daniel (2011), *Thinking Fast and Slow*, Penguin Group

[57] Kandampully, Jay and Suhartanto, Dwi (2000), *Customer loyalty in the hotel industry: the role of customer satisfaction and image*, International Journal of Contemporary Hospitality Management, vol 12 no 6, pg 346-351, MCB UP

[58] Kandampully, Jay (2006), *The new customer-centered business model for the hospitality industry*, International Journal of Contemporary Hospitality Management, vol 18 no 3, pg 173-187, Emerald Group Publishing Limited

[59] Keating, Mary and Harrington, Denis (2003), *The challenges of implementing quality in the Irish hotel industry*, Journal of European Industrial Training, vol 27 no 9, pg 441-453, MCB UP

[60] Kelly, Kevin (2016). *The Inevitable. Understanding the 12 Technological Forces That Will Shape Our Future*, US: Viking

[61] Kelly, Kevin (2014). The Three Breakthroughs That Have Finally Unleashed AI on the World, Retrieved from

https://www.wired.com/2014/10/future-of-artificial-intelligence/

[62] Kim, Larry (2018). *10 Remarketing Facts that Will Make You Rethink PPC*, Retrieved at

http://www.wordstream.com/blog/ws/2015/10/01/remarketing-facts

[63] Kiriakidou, Olivia and Millward, J Lynne (2000), *Corporate identity: external reality or internal fit?*, Corporate Communications: An International Journal, vol 5 no 1, pg 49-58, MCB UP

[64] Kirkup, Malcolm and Carrigan, Marylyn (200), *Video surveillance research in retailing: ethical issues*, International Journal of Retail & Distribution Management, vol 28 no 11, pg 470-480, MCB UP

[65] Klein, Gary (1998), *Sources of Power: How People Make Decisions*, Massachusetts Institute of Technology

[66] Krug, Steve (2014). *Don't Make Me Think. A Common Sense Approach To Web and Mobile Usability*, US: New Riders

[67] Lorsch, W Jay (1986), *Managing culture: The invisible barrier to Strategic Change*, California Management Review, vol 28 no 2, The Regents of the University of California

[68] Mailchimp (2018). *Marketing Automation is like a second brain for your business*, Retrieved at https://mailchimp.com/brain/#/

[69] Markwick, Nigel and Fill, Chris (1997), *Towards a framework for managing corporate identity*, European Journal of Marketing, vol 31 no 5:6, pg 396-409, MCB UP

[70] Marr, Bernard (2016). *Big Data in Practice. How 45 Successful Companies Used Big Data Analytics To Deliver Extraordinary Results*, GB: Wiley

[71] Marr, Bernard (2015). *Big Data. Using Smart Big Data Analytics And Metrics To Make Better Decisions And Improve Performance*, GB: Wiley

[72] Marvin, Ginny (2017). Google AdWords' automated ad suggestions test is getting a reboot, Retrieved at https://searchengineland.com/google-adwords-automated-ad-suggestions-beta-281924

McKinney, Wes (2016). *Python for Data Analysis*, US: O'Reilly Media

[73] Mei, Amy Wong Ooi; Dean, M Alison and White, J Christopher (1999), *Analyzing service quality in the hospitality industry*, Managing Service Quality, vol 9 no 2, pg 136-143, MCB UP

[74] Melewar, T.C. and Karaosmanoglu, Elif (2006), *Seven dimensions of corporate identity- A categorization from the practitioners' perspectives*, European Journal of Marketing, vol 40 no 7/8, pg 846-869, Emerald Group Publishing Limited

[75] Melewar, T.C; Basset, Kara and Simoes, Claudia (2006), *The role of communication and visual identity in modern organizations*, Corporate Communications: An International Journal, vol 11 no 2, pg 138-147, Emerald Group Publishing Limited

[76] Melewar, TC and Saunders, John (1998), *Global corporate visual identity systems: Standardization, control and benefits*, International Marketing Review, vol 15 no 4, pg 291-308, MCB UP

[77] Melewar, TC and Bains, Narinder (2002), *Industry in transition: corporate identity on hold?*; International Journal of Bank Marketing, vol 21 no 2, pg 57-66, MCB UP

[78] Min, Hokey; Min, Hyesung and Chung, Kyooyup (2002), *Dynamic benchmarking of hotel service quality*, Journal of Services Marketing, vol 16 no 4, pg 302-321, MCB UP

[79] Moingeon, Bertrand and Ramanantsoa, Bernard (1997), *Understanding corporate identity: the French school of thought*, European Journal of Marketing, vol 31 no 5/6, pg 383-395, MCB UP

[80] Moise, Imani (2018), *What's on Your Mind? Bosses Are Using Artificial Intelligence To Find Out,* Retrieved at https://www.wsj.com/articles/whats-on-your-mind-bosses-are-using-artificial-intelligence-to-find-out-1522251302

[81] Octopus HR, *Alphabet Case Study- Leading Car Leasing Firm Realises Enormous Benefits Using Octopus HR*, retrieved at http://www.octopus-hr.co.uk/docs/case/Alphabet%20Case%20Study.pdf

[82] Okumus, Fevzi and Hemmington, Nigel (1998), *Barriers and resistance to change in hotel firms: an investigation at unit level*, International Journal of Contemporary Hospitality Management, vol 10 no 7, pg 283-288, MCB UP

[83] Olins, Wally (1994), *Corporate identity*, Thames and Hudson

[84] Otubanjo, B Olutayo and Melewar, T.C. (2007), *Understanding the meaning of corporate identity: a conceptual and semiological approach*, Corporate Communications: An International Journal, vol 12 no 4, pg 414-432, Emerald Group Publishing Limited

[85] Padua, Laurie (2017), *The Rise of the AI Recruiter: Is HR tech the next to challenge human intuition?,* Retrieved from http://alexandermannsolutions.com/alexander-mann-solutions-live/news-item/the-rise-of-the-ai-recruiter-is-hr-tech-the-next-to-challenge-human-intuition

[86] Pink, H. Daniel (2009), *Drive. The Surprising truth about what motivates us*, Clays Ltd, St Ives Plc

[87] PMG (2018), *1st Franklin Financial Corporation Automates HR Processes along with Identity and Access Management,* Retrieved at http://www.pmg.net/wp-content/uploads/PMG-Case-Study-1FF.pdf

[88] Porter, Gayle (2004), *Work, work ethic, work excess*, Journal of Organizational Change Management, vol 17 no 5, pg 424-439, Emerald Group Publishing Limited

[89] Ramaswamy, Satya (2017), *How Companies Are Already Using AI,* Retrieved at https://hbr.org/2017/04/how-companies-are-already-using-ai

[90] Rashid, Md Zabid Abdul; Sambasivan, Murali and Rahman, Azmawani Abdul (2004), *The influence of organizational culture on attitudes towards organizational change*, The Leadership & Organization Development Journal, vol 25 no 2, pg 161-179, Emerald Group Publishing Limited

[91] Robertson, Ian (2012). *The Winner Effect. How Power Affects Your Brain*, GB: Bloomsbury

[92] Romano, Aja (2018). *The Facebook data breach wasn't a hack. It was a wake-up call,* Retrieved at https://www.vox.com/2018/3/20/17138756/facebook-data-breach-cambridge-analytica-explained

[93] Ross, Alec (2017). *The Industries of the Future*, UK: Simon & Schuster UK

[94] Ross, Lee & Nisbett, Richard E. (2011). *The Person And The Situation. Perspectives of Social Psychology*, GB: Pinter and Martin

[95] Rosten, April (2017), 2017 *Automation Nation Report: Recruiter Perspectives on an Automated Future,*

 Retrieved at https://www.jobvite.com/jobvite-news-and-reports/2017-automation-nation-report-recruiter-perspectives-automated-future/

[96] Rucinski, Daisy Arredondo and Bauch, A Patricia (2006), *Reflective, ethical, and moral constructs in educational leadership preparation: effects on graduates' practices, Journal of Educational Administration*, Journal of Educational Administration, vol 44 no 5, pg 487-508, Emerald Group Publishing Limited

[97] Scheeres, Hermine and Rhodes, Carl (2006), *Between cultures: values, training and identity in a manufacturing firm*, Journal of Organizational Change Management, vol 19 no 2, pg 223-236, Emerald Group Publishing Limited

[98] Schwartz, Howard and Davis, M. Stanley (1981), *Matching corporate culture and business strategy*, Organizational Dynamics, AMACOM

[99] Sennaar, Kumba (2017), *Machine Learning for Recruiting and Hiring – 6 Current Applications*, Retrieved at https://www.techemergence.com/machine-learning-for-recruiting-and-hiring/

[100] Sharot, Tali (2012), *The Optimism Bias*, Constable & Robinson Ltd

[101] Sharp, Byron (2010). *How brands Grow. What marketers don't know*, Australia: Oxford University Press

[102] Shanmugam, Abirami (2018), *From Sourcing to Hire: Artificial Intelligence (AI) in Recruiting*, Retrieved at https://www.zoho.com/recruit/blog/from-sourcing-to-hire-artificial-intelligence-ai-in-recruiting.html

[103] Sky,Nite (2015). *Virtual Reality Insider*, GB: Amazon

[104] Steele, M. Claude (2011), *Whistling Vivaldi: How Stereotypes Affect Us and What We Can Do*, President and Fellows of Harvard College

[105] Solnet, David (2006), *Introducing employee social identification to customer satisfaction research. A hotel industry study*; Managing Service Quality, vol 16 no 6, pg 575-594, Emerald Group Publishing Limited

[106] Suroviecki, James (2005), *The Wisdom of Crowds: Why the Many are Smarter than the Few*, Anchor Books

[107] Sutherland, Stuart (2007), *Irrationality*, Pinter & Martin Ltd

[108] Susskind, Richard & Susskind, Daniel (2017). *The Future Of Professions. How Technologies Will Transform The Work Of Human Experts*, GB: Oxford University Press

Stone, Brad (2013). *The Everything Store*, GB: Transworld Publishers

[109] Taleb, Nassim Nicholas (2007). *Fooled by Randomness. The Hidden Role of Chance in Life and in the Markets*, US: Penguin Books

[110] Tapscott, Don & Williams, Anthony D. (2006). *Wikinomics, How Mass Collaboration Changes Everything*, US: Portfolio

[1111] Tere, Rudolph (2008), *How to be an ethical researcher*,

URL: http://e-articles.info/e/a/title/How-to-be-an-Ethical-Researcher--Code-of-Ethics/

[22 Dec 2008]

[112] Tight, Malcolm; Blaxter, Loraine and Hughes, Christina (2001), *How to research*, *Second Edition*, Open University Press

[113] Topalian, Alan (2003), *Experienced reality: The development of corporate identity in the digital era*, European Journal of Marketing, vol 37 no 7/8, MCB UP

[114] Torres, N. Edwin and Kline, Sheryl (2006), *From satisfaction to delight: a model for the hotel industry*, International Journal of Contemporary Hospitality Management, vol 18 no 4, pg 290-301, Emerald Group Publishing Limited

[115] Totham, Isabel (2017).*10 Online Dating Statistics You Should Know*, Retrieved from **https://www.eharmony.com/online-dating-statistics/**

[116] Trivers, Robert (2011). *Deceit and Self-Deception. Fooling Yourself the Better to Fool Others*, GB: Allen Lane

[117] Trotman, Andrew (2014), *Facebook's Mark Zuckerberg: Why I wear the same T-shirt every day*, Retrieved from https://www.telegraph.co.uk/technology/facebook/11217273/Facebooks-Mark-Zuckerberg-Why-I-wear-the-same-T-shirt-every-day.html

Walton, Sam & Huey, John (1993). *Made In America*, US: Bantam

[118] Tsang, Nelson and Qu, Hailin (2000), *Service quality in China's hotel industry: a perspective from tourists and hotel managers*, International Journal of Contemporary Hospitality Management, vol 12 no 5, pg 316-326, MCB UP

[119] van Rekom, Johan (1997), *Deriving an operational measure of corporate identity*, European Journal of Marketing, vol 31 no 5:6, pg 410-422, MCB UP

[120] van Riel, BM Cees and Balmer, MT John (1997), *Corporate identity: the concept, its measurement and management*, European Journal of Marketing, vol 31 no 5/6, pg 340-355, MCB UP

[121]Verlinder, Neelie (2018), *Blockchain in HR: Challenges, Applications and the Future of Work*, retrieved at https://www.digitalhrtech.com/blockchain-hr-challenges-applications-future-of-work/

[122] Welch, Chris (2018). *Google just gave a stunning demo of Assistant making an actual phone call,* Retrieved from https://www.theverge.com/2018/5/8/17332070/google-assistant-makes-phone-call-demo-duplex-io-2018

[123] Whitwam, Ryan (2013), Simulating 1 second of human brain activity takes 82,944 processors, Retrieved from https://www.extremetech.com/extreme/163051-simulating-1-second-of-human-brain-activity-takes-82944-processors

[124] Wilkinson, Adrian and Balmer, MT John (1996), *Corporate and generic identities: lessons from the Co-operative Bank*, International Journal of Bank Marketing, vol 14 no 4, pg 22-35, MCB UP

[125] Wikipedia (2018). *Watson (computer)*. Retrieved at https://en.wikipedia.org/wiki/Watson_(computer)

[126] Wilson, D. Timothy (2011), *Redirect. The Surprising New Science of Psychological Change*, GB: Allen Lane

[127] Wilson, D. Timothy (2002), *Strangers to Ourselves. Discovering the adaptive unconscious*, GB: The Belknap Press of Harvard University Press

[128] Wiseman, Richard (2010). *:59 Seconds. Think a little, Change a lot*, GB: Pan Books

[129] Wiseman, Richard (2007). *Quirkology. The Curious Science Of Everyday Lives*, GB: Macmillan

[130] Workday (2018), *Workday and TalkTalk Discovering the power of one*, Retrieved at https://www.workday.com/content/dam/web/uk/documents/case-studies/casestudy-talktalk-uk.pdf

[131] York, Alex (2018). *61 Social Media Statistics to Bookmark for 2018*. Retrieved at https://sproutsocial.com/insights/social-media-statistics/

9 781999 622541